RECOVERING EDEN

THE GOSPEL ACCORDING TO
THE OLD TESTAMENT

*A series of studies on the lives
of Old Testament characters, written for
laypeople and pastors, and designed to
encourage Christ-centered reading, teaching,
and preaching of the Old Testament*

IAIN M. DUGUID
Series Editor

RECOVERING EDEN

THE GOSPEL ACCORDING TO
ECCLESIASTES

ZACK ESWINE

P&R
PUBLISHING
P.O. BOX 817 • PHILLIPSBURG • NEW JERSEY 08865-0817

ISBN: 978-1-59638-468-2 (pbk)
ISBN: 978-1-59638-649-5 (ePub)
ISBN: 978-1-59638-650-1 (Mobi)

Printed in the United States of America

Library of Congress Cataloging-in-Publication Data

Eswine, Zack, 1969-
  Recovering Eden : the gospel according to Ecclesiastes / Zack Eswine. -- 1st ed.
       pages cm. -- (The Gospel according to the Old Testament)
  Includes bibliographical references and index.
  ISBN 978-1-59638-468-2 (pbk.)
  1. Bible. Ecclesiastes--Criticism, interpretation, etc. 2. Christian life--Biblical teaching. I. Title.
  BS1475.6.C43E89 2013
  223'.806--dc23
                                                   2013010732

For Jessica, Nathan, Abigail, and Caleb

The days of darkness will be many,
but light is sweet,
and it is pleasant to see the sun.

Ecclesiastes 11:7–8

CONTENTS

FOREWORD

The New Testament is in the Old concealed;
the Old Testament is in the New revealed.
—Augustine

Concerning this salvation, the prophets who prophesied about the grace that was to be yours searched and inquired carefully, inquiring what person or time the Spirit of Christ in them was indicating when he predicted the sufferings of Christ and the subsequent glories. It was revealed to them that they were serving not themselves but you, in the things that have now been announced to you through those who preached the good news to you by the Holy Spirit sent from heaven, things into which angels long to look. (1 Peter 1:10–12)

"Moreover, some women of our company amazed us. They were at the tomb early in the morning, and when they did not find his body, they came back saying that they had even seen a vision of angels, who said that he was alive. Some of those who were with us went to the tomb and found it just as the women had said, but him they did not see." And he said to them, "O foolish ones, and slow of heart to believe all that the prophets have spoken! Was it not necessary that the Christ should suffer these things and enter into his glory?" And beginning with Moses and all the Prophets, he interpreted to them in all the Scriptures the things concerning himself. (Luke 24:22–27)

The prophets searched. Angels longed to see. And the disciples didn't understand. But Moses, the Prophets, and all the Old Testament Scriptures had spoken about it—that Jesus would come, suffer, and then be glorified. God began to tell a story in the Old Testament, the ending of which the audience eagerly anticipated. But the Old Testament audience was left hanging. The plot was laid out, but the climax was delayed. The unfinished story begged for an ending. In Christ, God has provided the climax to the Old Testament story. Jesus did not arrive unannounced; his coming was declared *in advance* in the Old Testament—not just in explicit prophecies of the Messiah, but also by means of the stories of all the events, characters, and circumstances in the Old Testament. God was telling a larger, overarching, unified story. From the account of creation in Genesis to the final stories of the return from exile, God progressively unfolded his plan of salvation. And the Old Testament account of that plan always pointed in some way to Christ.

AIMS OF THIS SERIES

The Gospel According to the Old Testament series was begun by my former professors, Tremper Longman and Al Groves, to whom I owe an enormous personal debt of gratitude. I learned from them a great deal about how to recognize the gospel in the Old Testament. I share their deep conviction that the Bible, both Old and New Testaments, is a unified revelation of God and that its thematic unity is found in Christ. This series of studies will continue to pursue their initial aims:

- to lay out the pervasiveness of the revelation of Christ in the Old Testament

- to promote a Christ-centered reading of the Old Testament
- to encourage Christ-centered preaching and teaching from the Old Testament

These volumes are written primarily for pastors and laypeople, not scholars. They are designed in the first instance to serve the church, not the academy.

My hope and prayer remain the same as Tremper and Al's: that this series will continue to encourage the revival of interest in the Old Testament as a book that constantly points forward to Jesus Christ, to his sufferings and the glories that would follow.

IAIN M. DUGUID

ACKNOWLEDGMENTS

I am grateful for the partnership of Iain Duguid with his time, editorial skill, and love for God as he reveals himself in the Old Testament. I give thanks for Marvin Padgett and the staff at P&R Publishing for this opportunity to meditate on God through this wild and strange wonder called Ecclesiastes.

I also continue to learn the gospel from the congregation of Riverside Church, here in Webster Groves, Missouri. Their partnership in affording me friendship, time, editorial help, and daily gospel encouragement for my life and ministry makes writing this book possible.

CHAPTER ONE

AN UNEXPECTED VOICE

"A long moan answers, rising in our talk."[1]

hen readers in the early 1960s first perused the book *A Grief Observed*, many found comfort but some felt troubled. The troubled ones were accustomed to hearing solid strength, strong faith, formidable apologetics, and credible worship from the pen of C. S. Lewis. Suddenly now, to read his doubts and questions so raw and transparent was unusual, strange, and befuddling. This widower's voice, like his aging head, his dripping nose, and his heaving shoulders, leaned heavy onto the chest of the page, and some who held him there as they read his grieving words became restless, frightened, and disconcerted. "It doesn't really matter whether you grip the arms of the dentist's chair or let your hands lie in your lap," Lewis wrote. "The drill drills on."[2]

> Talk to me about the truth of religion and I'll listen gladly. Talk to me about the duty of religion and I'll listen submissively. But don't come talking to me about the consolations of religion or I shall suspect that you don't understand.[3]

> Meanwhile, where is God? . . . Go to him when your need is desperate, when all other help is vain, and

what do you find? A door slammed in your face, and a sound of bolting and double bolting on the inside. After that, silence. You may as well turn away. The longer you wait, the more emphatic the silence will become.[4]

Lewis's readers did not expect someone like that to talk like this. The book sat on their shelves next to *Mere Christianity*, *The Great Divorce*, *The Problem of Pain*, and *The Weight of Glory*, but some felt less certain about their desire to read it and how or if they were meant to use it.

Many people who cherish the Bible express a similar reaction to the book of Ecclesiastes. We do not expect the words we find there. What many of us have come to expect from the Bible in general and this messenger in particular, doesn't match. Yet, the same God who inspired the Psalms and the Gospels speaks here too. These inspired words which disturb us reveal aspects of God too often neglected by us. If one has only driven a car with automatic transmission, driving manually will take some getting used to. What do we need to know in order to "get used to" the way this book functions in its attempt to get us from one place to another?

SEEKING DOUBLE KNOWLEDGE

The pastor and theologian John Calvin believed that we discover wisdom and life by means of double knowledge: the knowledge of God and of ourselves.[5] Accordingly, if we want to know God, we must learn moment by moment to furnish our mind with the contemplation of God.

The books of the Bible invite us to this double knowledge. Some books, like Romans, put God center stage. We learn about him mostly by contemplating him directly and less by paying attention to ourselves.

But one of the ways that God leads us to know him is by making us pay attention to ourselves. He reveals himself by recovery of our humanity. He shows us what we were made for and then bids us to look at what has become of us. This is what you will want to admit about Ecclesiastes. In the same way as books such as Ruth or Esther, in Ecclesiastes God intends you to know him by requiring you to look plainly and without polish at yourself, your neighbors, and the world in which you and I live. God puts himself in the background, as it were, in order to place self-concern front and center.

"We are prompted by our own ills," says Calvin, "to contemplate the good things of God."[6] In the Spirit's hands, Ecclesiastes confronts us with our own ills in order that by knowing ourselves as we are we might come to know God as he is.

THE PERSPECTIVE OF THIS VOICE

The one whom God has designated to tell us about ourselves is "the Preacher" (Eccl. 1:1). The word translated "Preacher" refers to "the gathering or assembly of a community of people, especially for the worship of God."[7] Therefore, the king of Israel, the son of David, is "like a pastor in a church,"[8] preaching. In that light, Ecclesiastes "is a sermon with a text ('vanity of vanities,' 1:2; 12:8)," an explanation of that text (Eccl. 1–10), and an application of what that text then means for our lives (Eccl. 11:1–12:7).[9] But this sermon unsettles immediately, for what the Preacher does is step to his pulpit and shout at us, "Vanity! Everything is vanity!" (see Eccl. 1:2).

But this Preacher-king takes up the title "son of David" and identifies himself as the heir to the psalm-singing, sling-shot-hurling, shepherd-king, whom God said was "a man after his own heart" (1 Sam. 13:14). Even more, "son of David" signifies the mantle that God's promise would in time place upon Jesus (Matt. 1:1). Such credentials promote our expectation of a powerful and uplifting biblical

3

sermon. Yet, the Preacher-king steps up to his pulpit and tells us that what God gives us in this life amounts to little more than "an unhappy business" (Eccl. 1:13).

Furthermore, Ecclesiastes lets us hear the voice of an older pastor/disciple-maker. He is a sage mentor speaking to his students not only as a giver of words, but also as a companion for living so that the young can learn (Eccl. 12:1). Like the wise before him (Prov. 23:26), and the apostles after him (2 Tim. 2:1), and Jesus with his followers (John 13:33), we are to hear the Preacher too, as offering affectionate speech, like a spiritual father instructing his dearly loved spiritual children (Eccl. 12:11).

Similarly, like David the king who preceded him (Ps. 23) and the Lord who came after him (John 10:11), we are meant to hear the Preacher's words as if we who listen are a flock under the care of one Shepherd (Eccl. 12:11). He intends that we will hear something resonant with the voice of this one Shepherd in the midst of his human voice. We are surprised then when this sage mentor tells us that he "hated life" (Eccl. 2:17) and that gaining wisdom and knowledge does nothing but stress us out and make us sad (Eccl. 1:18).

Like those who were bothered by C. S. Lewis's book on grief, we too might wonder how a spokesman for God could talk like this in God's name and whether or not we should listen to a preacher who sermonizes in this way. We might think to ourselves, "This guy just doesn't sound like Isaiah, Jeremiah, or John or Peter. More importantly, he doesn't sound like Jesus."[10]

These thoughts make sense when we recognize that the Preacher of Ecclesiastes offers a different category of sermon than what Isaiah, Jeremiah, John, or Peter offered to us. (We will come back to the question of whether or not the Preacher sounds like Jesus in a moment.) Most of us have not encountered this kind of wisdom preaching or sage pastoral perspective before. So, we do not know what to make of it. Like an American driver in New

Zealand, we need to switch our sights to a different side of the road than we are used to and to a different vantage point in the car, in order to navigate these opposite streets. Sometimes making this switch takes a little time and feels quite scary.

A WISDOM VOICE

Making this switch begins with recognizing what kind of terrain we are traveling. The neighborhoods of Ecclesiastes are filled with wisdom streets. Many Christians have grown up traveling the prophetic roads of the Old Testament and the Pauline highways of the New Testament. Wisdom highways are less traveled. The Song of Solomon is like a back-road brothel to us. (As a young man, I was told by a pastor not to read this book until after I was married!) Job is like a long stretch of desert road with no night light and no gas stations or rest stops for miles. People can get stuck out there with no help, so we rarely travel there without a great deal of preparation. James is like an old law building that doesn't seem to fit the gospel landscape. We drive around it and wonder if we should bulldoze it. Ecclesiastes sounds like a crazed man downtown. He smells like he hasn't bathed—looks like it too—and as we pass by he won't stop glaring at us and beckoning to us that our lives are built on illusions, and that we are all going to die. So, most of us choose to get our lunch at a different shop on a less dreary corner of town. Meanwhile, we usually like our visits to the Psalms, except for the ones that we feel we need to rewrite or edit because of how uncomfortably raw the emotions they express are. Their moodiness can ruin a good time.

In short, most who have grown up in the Christian community have very little acquaintance with the neighborhoods of wisdom. The wisdom books are like those neighbors at which we smile but with whom we rarely converse because they live on the "other side of the tracks." No wonder Ecclesiastes sounds foreign to us.

But, as J. I. Packer once said, "The Bible is God preaching."[11] Though this voice in Ecclesiastes is strange for many of us to hear, the biblical Wisdom Literature reminds us that God (unlike many of us) has not been squeamish about speaking with riddles, maxims, metaphors, or poetry to his people. God has not been afraid of transparency, mystery, emotion, appeals to nature, or an intimate familiarity with the beauties and messes of people and things.[12] Like two acquaintances who as they get to know each other say, "I didn't know you could talk like that," the biblical Wisdom Literature in general, and Ecclesiastes in particular, show us more of God than perhaps we knew or are comfortable with.

VOICING THE EXCEPTIONS

As we think about this wisdom approach, we can meditate on the fact that if Proverbs focuses on the norms and rules, "Ecclesiastes focuses on the exceptions."[13] As students, many of us hate learning about exceptions. It takes so much effort just to learn the rules. When we finally do master the rules, the teacher then says, "It does not always work according to the rule you've just learned."

For example, as a child learning how to spell in English, it can take a while to learn the helpful rule that "*i* comes before *e*." This rule helps us to correctly spell words like *believe* or *grieve*. We receive a gold star on the spelling paper that suggests we've mastered the rule. But then, the teacher introduces words such as *neither* or *neighbor* or *receive*. She then writes down several exceptions for us to learn. She expands the rule to account for exceptions and says, "*I* before *e* except after *c* and sometimes *y* and in words that sound like *a* such as neighbor and weigh." A student who cannot overcome her impatience with the exceptions and who remains hasty to avoid anything but the rule will struggle to spell. So it is in life.

The Wisdom Literature needs Ecclesiastes then, in order to keep us from entrusting ourselves to trite formulas under the sun. It is not that Proverbs ignores exceptions. It too makes plain that rules aren't enough and that context matters for how we apply wisdom.

> Answer not a fool according to his folly,
>   lest you be like him yourself.
> Answer a fool according to his folly,
>   lest he be wise in his own eyes. (Prov. 26:4–5)

But our recurring inability as human beings to deal in more than just appearances with God and with our neighbors reveals our strong need for the Preacher's sermon in Ecclesiastes. For example, Proverbs teaches us a principle. "Disaster pursues sinners, but the righteous are rewarded with good" (Prov. 13:21). In this light, "Job's friends seem warranted in their assessment of Job's condition. . . . What else is there then but that Job needs to repent?"[14] His disaster reveals to everyone that he has sinned. Yet, the Preacher in Ecclesiastes tells us an exception "under the sun."

> In my vain life I have seen everything. There is a righteous man who perishes in his righteousness, and there is a wicked man who prolongs his life in his evildoing. (Eccl. 7:15)

Contrary to how his religious friends interpreted him, Job was actually a righteous man. The story of "Job illustrates the sort of thing for which Ecclesiastes is preparing his students. The difficulty that arose between Job and his friends did so because Job's experience did not correspond to the standard categories."[15] It's as if Job's friends knew a proverbial rule that "*i* comes before *e*," but they had no category for "after *c* or sometimes *y* or with sounds of *a* like neighbor and weigh." Therefore, they misapplied true things and damaged their neighbor instead of loving him—and all of this, they did misguidedly in God's name.

Ecclesiastes echoes and foreshadows this recurring temptation. After all, Jesus' disciples were no different. When a man was born blind they assumed that this disaster was caused by sin, his own or his parents'. Jesus let them know that they were mistaken (John 9:1-3). When some were murdered in a political coup or when a tower fell and several were tragically killed, the disciples assumed that those who died did so because they were worse sinners than others (Luke 13:1-5). Jesus let them know that he sees things differently than that.

Similarly, Ecclesiastes offers an exceptional voice to remind us who are like Job's friends or Jesus' disciples that we cannot walk out into our neighborhoods under the sun and hand out a "one size fits all" shirt. Life under the sun isn't that tidy. Contradictions abound with human beings and the world. The Preacher does not shy away from these. We are prone to clean our house before guests arrive. The Preacher doesn't. He lets the house remain as it is. He asks us to see it and to ponder what it reveals about us, our place, and God.

By taking up this untidy voice, the Preacher isn't using this sermon to describe life as we expect it, or as he desires it or as what good theology says that life should be. Rather the Preacher describes life as it actually presents itself "under the sun." If someone were to say to him, "You shouldn't talk about such things," it is as if he responds, "But people already go through this kind of stuff and have to talk about it under the sun." If someone were to say to him, "The things you talk about shouldn't happen," it is as if he says, "No, they shouldn't, but they do, so now what?" Therefore, "without question, Ecclesiastes regularly points out things that many people in the church prefer not to acknowledge."[16] The Preacher does not stick to the rules of what should be but addresses the exceptions to account for what is.

We would be remiss, however, if we thought of this Preacher as only dealing in exceptions and contradictions. On the contrary, Ecclesiastes teaches us plenty of norms (Eccl. 7). But most of these norms are of a different kind. More often than not, these norms have to do, not with didactic principles, but with the kinds of circumstances and situations or "seasons" that one must navigate under the sun. If Proverbs is like math, mostly dealing in equations in which one thing adds up to equal another, then Ecclesiastes is like music, all mood with melody and tone. If Proverbs is like meteorology giving us indicators so as to predict certain outcomes, then Ecclesiastes is like the actual weather, fickle and unpredictable in its ability to rant with storms or breathe easy with a mid-morning breeze. In Proverbs a good man plus God's love and wisdom equals a good life. In Ecclesiastes a good man plus God's love still dies like the beast or the fool. In Proverbs, wisdom gives us eyes to recognize the storm clouds and what to do in response. In Ecclesiastes, death is a piece of tornado from which no proverbial basement can shelter us.

For this reason, the Preacher is a skeptic but of the kind commended in the Scripture. Unlike folly, this Preacher does not rush in to accept the first thing he sees or hears. He is no simpleton. He is not naive like those who do not ponder the path of life. These wander but do not know it (Prov. 5:6).

Instead, the heart of the wise thinks through their ways of doing life (Prov. 4:26). It "ponders how to answer" (Prov. 15:28) because it has come to learn that "there is a way that seems right to a man, but its end is the way of death" (Prov. 14:12). Therefore the wise take a posture that examines, waits, listens, hears the best arguments, and gives time to search out what is presented without minimizing or exaggerating or denying it.

> The one who states his case first seems right,
> until the other comes and examines him.
> (Prov. 18:17)

If he is a pessimist, he is so as one who believes that God and truth remain. This kind of skepticism is rare for many of us and therefore strange to our experience.

A WISDOM KIND OF OUTREACH

Our discomfort with this Preacher's voice also rises because, like Job and Proverbs, the Preacher of Ecclesiastes does not require us who listen to possess explicit Bible knowledge. Unlike most other books in the Bible, here, there is no mention of Abraham, or Moses or David or the coming Messiah, or the history of Israel. A person with no knowledge of the Bible can sit in the pew as this Preacher speaks, and they can feel that he is using their language to speak about things that they themselves know. In fact, "strikingly absent" from this Preacher's message "are the great themes of biblical history, such as the exodus, covenant and the conquest of the land. God's role as deliverer and lawgiver, in turn, is scarcely mentioned."[17] "Ecclesiastes does not focus on God's redemptive acts."[18]

For those who are accustomed to sermons that purpose to "get us saved," or that are filled with phrases such as, "God says," or "the Bible says," Ecclesiastes is strange. If we are accustomed to hearing sermons given by preachers who speak formally rather than personally, in churches that see asking questions as a lack of faith, among Christians who see reading poetry, stories, and riddles as a waste of time, with a mindset that believers are not to be in the secular world, this book in the Bible can baffle, flabbergast, and even infuriate us. This Preacher is no old-school evangelist from the American South or Midwest. His kind of relationship with God and neighbor is older still. His approach is new to many of us, not because his way of doing ministry is newfangled, but because it is so old and wise as to be forgotten.

His approach makes central his humanity rather than his faith, his creatureliness rather than his redemption. Ecclesiastes starts decidedly with the truth that all of us are in the world no matter who we are and that all of us have this one thing in common: we are human and as such we must commonly navigate the same God-governed and maddening world together. The Preacher speaks, not so much as a Jewish believer, then, but as a human being. He recovers a sense of our common humanity.

Centuries later the apostle Paul would sometimes preach his own sermons in like fashion. Of course, when he spoke in the synagogue among those who knew the Scriptures, Paul preached of the promised deliverer, the history of Israel, and our own hearts in that light. He quoted explicitly from the Bible and spoke explicitly of Jesus (Acts 13:16–41).

But, standing up before a crowd of people who knew nothing about the Hebrew Scriptures or of the God to which they point us, Paul could take the culture and not the Bible for his text. He could quote their own poets rather than the Scriptures to introduce them to God. He could speak, not of the Redeemer of Israel, but of the Creator and sustainer of the world, who has sent someone to us and has raised him from the dead. Paul can preach in such contexts without mentioning the explicit name of Jesus (Acts 14:8–18; 17:22–31). Then, as some wanted to talk more in these settings, Paul would gladly do so and go further (Acts 17:32).

Perhaps it can help us to think about Ecclesiastes as an incomplete forerunner to this kind of Pauline sermon. This kind of sermon introduces but does not answer everything. After we hear it, we want to talk further and grapple more deeply with what we've just heard.

Like Paul when he was among neighbors without the Bible, this Preacher in Ecclesiastes, who looks at the world from the vantage point of the Scriptures, chooses nonetheless neither to open them up nor to expound explicitly from them as we gather to hear him preach. Not this time. Instead, he chooses the cultural experiences and texts from our being human under the sun, and from there, as one of us, he tells us about the God who created us and governs the world. With Paul, this Preacher believes that we will stand before God after we die and give an account of our lives (Eccl. 3:17; 11:9; 12:14). But unlike Paul, the Preacher in Ecclesiastes does not answer us about the resurrection. Instead, this Preacher joins us in the search for the answer (Eccl. 3:21). He is a fellow human being interrogating the world and our experience. He recognizes the limits of our knowledge and the real questions that nag us. In this light, he does not give voice to the most trite of human objections about God and the world. Rather, he gives voice to true human angst.

Therefore, as we who believe in the God of the Bible hear him, this Preacher can apprentice us. We can learn how a follower of God is meant to talk to the world about the world as a fellow human being. We learn a wisdom kind of outreach, an evangelism or testimony as those who are human beings wrestling with it all. It is as if the Preacher causes us to put off our religious persona and get honest about our being human in a fallen world.

Likewise, as we who do not believe in God hear this Preacher, we cannot help but resonate with the credibility, the honesty, the humanity, the wisdom of what he says. For what he says rings true to what is there in the world and within us.

Consequently, whether we believe or not, as human beings we can access Ecclesiastes and hear our questions and our culture's answers on the Preacher's tongue. We feel our lament in his pain. We see our own tantrums in his frustrations. We touch our own longings as he cries out with his. The Preacher gives language to our ache, poetry for our dreams, and exclamation for our search. He resists anything trite, pretentious, sentimental, or dishonest. By this means, the God who inspired this text shows us his empathy and his profound understanding of our plight in all of its confusing, emotional, tragic, and maddening forms.

In this light, the Preacher-pastor has an apologetic aim. An apologist is one who gives a defense or reason for the faith (1 Peter 3:15). Ecclesiastes is an apologetic sermon. Like "an essay in apologetics . . . it defends a life of faith in a generous God by pointing to the grimness of the alternative."[19]

For this reason (to borrow a phrase from Francis Schaeffer), Ecclesiastes can apprentice us in what it means to communicate as a human being with "the man without the Bible."[20] He models for us how a student or disciple who seeks to follow God can engage our neighbors as human beings under the sun. Therefore, as you prepare to read his message, the Preacher will not preach at you with unquestioning rhetorical polish as an expert. Instead he will humble himself in your presence, share his own intimate questions about life with you, and reach out for God with you, as he too is a fellow human being. Most of us have rarely encountered this kind of preacher with this kind of approach. Many of us have little idea of how to jettison our religious language and garb and to humble ourselves in creaturely ways as we sweat together with our neighbors on this parched earth.

The Preacher shows us how. From him we learn to listen; to represent without spin how people think, feel, and act; to admit that we ourselves must weather the same conditions, and that we too long to recover for ourselves a credible and honest answer to what troubles us.

RECOVERING EDEN

Sometimes answering what troubles us takes us back to first things.

On one occasion for example, the apostle Paul and Barnabas found themselves confronted by the beliefs and interpretations of those around them. When those from the culture of Lystra saw God's power in these preachers, they interpreted them from their own cultural way of thinking. "The gods have come down to us," these neighbors shouted. "Barnabas they called Zeus, and Paul, Hermes, because he was the chief speaker" (Acts 14:11–12).

Paul and Barnabas responded in a threefold way. First, they proclaimed their humanity and related as human beings to those who heard them. "We also are men, of like nature with you," they cried out (Acts 14:15). Second, they stated that they were bearers of a good message that they had to share with those in Lystra (Acts 14:15). Third, they spoke, not about Jesus (not yet), but about "a living God who made the heaven and the earth and the sea and all that is in them" (Acts 14:15).

In past generations he allowed all the nations to walk in their own ways. Yet he did not leave himself without witness, for he did good by giving you rains from heaven and fruitful seasons, satisfying your hearts with food and gladness. (Acts 14:16–17)

For people who interpret life without the Bible and who do not know about the God whom that Bible reveals, Paul points to the "witness" that God has given us as human beings. This divine witness attends creaturely things such as rain, farming, and fruitful labor. Our life and work can offer a pleasantness to our hearts and we can enjoy our food, and by implication the toil that produced it, with gladness.

A witness is someone who gives testimony to what they have seen, heard, or personally experienced. Paul reminds us that creation and our lot within it to work, harvest, eat, and enjoy what we've been given is itself a witness in the world, testifying to us about the existence and character of God toward us.

In an analogous way, the Preacher in Ecclesiastes seems to have this same kind of purpose in mind. This Preacher also interacts with how people in the world interpret God. He too takes our common humanity as his starting place. He too has a message, and this message has to do with the witness of our lot with God. This witness is his apologetic.

The phrase "There is nothing better" travels powerfully off this Preacher's lips as he states his convictions. His wisdom compels us to compare our response to his. What would we say is the best good in this hassled life? For the Preacher, the best good in life is that we have work, family, and food in a place to enjoy.

> There is nothing better for a person than that he should eat and drink and find enjoyment in his toil. This also, I saw, is from the hand of God, for apart from him who can eat or who can have enjoyment? (Eccl. 2:24–25)

> There is nothing better for them than to be joyful and to do good as long as they live; also that everyone should eat and drink and take pleasure in all his toil—this is God's gift to man. (Eccl. 3:12–13)

> There is nothing better than that a man should rejoice in his work, for that is his lot. (Eccl. 3:22)

In other words, the best good in the madness under the sun is found when we recover some small resemblance to what we were made for in Eden. We remember that God's gift to humanity has not quit, even though we have and the world now groans. We remember Adam and Eve's season prior to their fall, and we learn again to long for that recovery while we are migrants here, worn out among the shanties.

We hear him tell us that "God made man upright, but they have sought out many schemes" (Eccl. 7:29). But though our many schemes sabotaged life under the sun, the gift of having a place to dwell, a thing to do, sustenance to cultivate, and a people to enjoy it with has not left us. God, and this witness to him, remains.

So, in a manner not so different from some of Paul's preaching, "there are clear connections between Ecclesiastes and the beginning of redemptive history as recounted in the early chapters of Genesis."[21] In fact, "it would seem that the Preacher is drawing on the themes of these Genesis chapters and is pressing home their implications" to us.[22]

God created us. His good gifts remain for us and for our joy. Counterfeit gifts, forged advantages, and illusory pleasures now abound like weeds bent on choking out the flowerbed. Everything is without meaning now. But there are these flowers that still bloom, these leftover beauties that do not quit. These small voices give witness still to the moaning world.

AN EVANGELISTIC HINT

What does this mean but that as a preacher/sage mentor/apologist this book brings with it an evangelistic hint? An evangelist is one who declares and commends his beliefs to others in the hope that they will convert from their ways to the ways commended by the evangelist. The Preacher in Ecclesiastes similarly hopes that the one hearing his message will believe it, convert to it, and leave the unsatisfactory paths that damage it. He hopes to convert us to his way as "a skilled craftsman in the art of teaching and persuasion."[23]

Besides being wise, the Preacher also taught the people knowledge, weighing and studying and arranging many proverbs with great care. The Preacher

sought to find words of delight, and uprightly he
wrote words of truth. (Eccl. 12:9–10)

In this light, his ramblings are not haphazard. Behind
the strangeness of this sermon resides a thorough study,
an intentional craft, and a commitment to confront those
listening hearers with the gift of God. Even more, the aim
of this Preacher's message is that we who listen will come
to believe in God and to recover our purpose with his gift
and to see that our whole purpose as human beings is a
God-centered relationship toward all things. This Preacher
hopes to persuade us to recognize that God is the one to
whom we belong and in whom we must place our trust.
God's ways and words as spoken in the Scriptures identify
the ways and words that the Preacher longs for us to take
up. The Preacher ultimately wants us to believe that evil
and good are real, that our sins in secret will be found out,
and that along with those who've sinned against us we
all will give an account of our lives to God. In fact, even
under the sun, with its madness, unanswered questions,
exceptions, contradictions, and vain striving, the whole
purpose or duty of one's life is still God himself.

The end of the matter; all has been heard. Fear God
and keep his commandments, for this is the whole
duty of man. For God will bring every deed into
judgment, with every secret thing, whether good
or evil. (Eccl. 12:13–14)

WHO IS THIS PREACHER?

When C. S. Lewis first published *A Grief Observed*, he
did so by veiling not only his own name but also by veiling
the name of his wife, Joy. He identified himself as N. W.
Clerk and referred to her as "H." After his death, the book
was published in his own name. Why would someone

17

publish under a pseudonym? Mary Anne Evans authored her famed books by using the name George Eliot, so that people could seriously receive her work amid the male-dominant reality of her generation. For Lewis, the kind of attention he received publicly made anonymity desirable as he was still living out the raw and personal account of his own life. We do not know why the writer of Ecclesiastes veils his real name and instead writes under the pen name "the Preacher." But the fact that he does has meant that people differ regarding who they think this Preacher is.

Historically, Christians have recognized the author of Ecclesiastes as Solomon. Who else could say, "I have acquired great wisdom surpassing all who were in Jerusalem before me?" (Eccl. 1:16; see 1 Kings 3:12–13). Furthermore, Solomon is the actual son of David, the king of Israel, and what the Preacher describes about wisdom, riches, and pleasures mirrors Solomon's own life. There is also this strong hint of identity located in the parallel phrases.

> The proverbs of Solomon, son of David, king of Israel. (Prov. 1:1)
> The words of the Preacher, the son of David, king in Jerusalem. (Eccl. 1:1)

But because he does not mention his name, many Bible scholars now suggest otherwise. Their contrary assumption states that if Solomon wrote this book, he would plainly say so. But Solomon is a human being like any other. As we have seen, sometimes writers have purposes for changing or veiling their names.

Others point out that it seems strange for a king to say things, for example, that criticize wealthy kings who oppress the poor (Eccl. 5:8). Yet, this too is inconclusive. After all, the writings of Israel differ from the spin that other kings and histories write for themselves. The Old Testament repeatedly shows us the foibles, follies, and sins of even its best kings. Theologically, the one writing Ecclesiastes does so as the appointed king for God's people. It does not surprise that a righteous king will therefore join in with the rest of the Scripture's teaching to condemn oppression of the poor, in contrast to kings like Ahab who in their history cared little for the poor and acted unjustly in God's name. King David rebuked the misuse of the innocent and the poor by the wealthy, not realizing that he thereby condemned himself. Upon realizing this, the king of Israel publicly repented. By doing so, he showed God's people that how he had acted as king was wrong and not for imitation by those who follow God (2 Sam. 12). It is just as plausible therefore that Ecclesiastes and Solomon simply follow this biblical pattern.

Still others wrestle with the different voices in the book. A good bit of the book is written from the standpoint of a first-person author, like the giving of one's testimony. The Preacher says things like, "I said in my heart," or "I applied my heart." But in Ecclesiastes 12:9ff, the voice shifts, and the words of the Preacher are spoken of in the third person. This view suggests that it seems odd that a person should speak of himself in the third person. Therefore, there must be at least two authors for the book. Either one of them or neither of them is Solomon. However, this too is inconclusive. For example, the apostle Paul will at times shift from first person to third person speech about himself (2 Cor. 12:1–5). This rhetorical move is not unheard of.

My point is that credible reasons are offered either way. Though I lean toward the now-minority view that Solomon is the actual author of this book, for our purposes we will follow J. I. Packer's sound advice in our approach.

Whether this means that Solomon himself was the preacher, or that the preacher put his sermon into Solomon's mouth as a didactic device . . . need not concern us. The sermon is certainly Solomonic in the sense that it teaches lessons which Solomon had unique opportunities to learn.[24]

Solomon's strong identity, story, and unique opportunities to learn what the Preacher here addresses will form the backdrop for this unexpected voice.

CONCLUSION

In his grief, Lewis wrestled plainly with two seeming contradictions. The first has to do with the felt absence of God, our illusions about him, and the unsettling frankness of our speaking of it.

> Not that I am (I think) in much danger of ceasing to believe in God. The real danger is of coming to believe such dreadful things about him. The conclusion I dread is not, "So there's no God after all," but "So this is what God's really like. Deceive yourself no longer."[25]

The second has to do with the presence of God that comes in a quality that we do not expect in order to meet desires that we cannot deny we have. In terms of desire, Lewis admits that in his love for Joy, "no cranny of heart or body remained unsatisfied." And yet, he says,

> We both knew that we wanted something besides one another—quite a different kind of something, a quite different kind of want. You might as well say that when lovers have one another they will never want to read, or eat—or breathe.[26]

And yet, Lewis acknowledges that God does not answer his questions. While earlier in the book he described God as silent behind a double-locked door, later he speaks differently about how unexpectedly God's silence is "not the locked door" as we imagine it to be.

> It is more like a silent, certainly not uncompassionate, gaze. As though He shook His head not in refusal but waiving the question. Like, "Peace, child; you don't understand."[27]

The Preacher in Ecclesiastes wrestles too. As a sage mentor for his students, he makes an apologetic case with an evangelistic hint for our recovery of what is truly good— the recovery of a resonance with Eden's gift with God. But he too is human. He too listens for the answer to his questions on this side of the locked door.

QUESTIONS FOR DISCUSSION

1. If Ecclesiastes is like a sermon, how does this sermon differ from the kinds we normally hear from our pastors? What do these differences teach us about the way God sometimes preaches to us?
2. Ecclesiastes causes us to resist formulaic approaches to life with God. Discuss why Ecclesiastes matters to us in light of Proverbs or how Job's friends related to Job.
3. What do you make of the idea of double knowledge? How does knowing ourselves help us to know God?
4. What is a "wisdom kind of outreach"? How does this kind of outreach differ from the kind of evangelism or defense of the faith that you are used to hearing?
5. How does Ecclesiastes resemble some of the apostle Paul's sermons?
6. How does Ecclesiastes relate to the book of Genesis? What do we mean when we say that in some ways the Preacher is recovering Eden in Ecclesiastes?

CHAPTER TWO

AN UNEXPECTED METHOD

"In the long winter nights, the farmer's dreams
are narrow.
Over and over he enters the furrow."[1]

We continue our introduction to this book with an analogy.

When you go to a park, you talk to a park ranger. The park ranger knows the location of every path. He knows where you're supposed to be by sunset as well as where danger lies if you attempt an after-sunset walkabout. You need the park ranger in order to navigate the park.

Or similarly, consider the tour guide driving his bus through a historic site, "Over here on your left you'll see such and so," the guide will say. The tour guide's experience of the place enables you with his help to properly name what you see out your window. It is like a large map inside the door of a suburban mall. "You are here," it shows you. By such a mark you locate yourself in relation to every hallway or store in the building. Every book of the Bible resembles these analogies, but Ecclesiastes particularly so. Ecclesiastes determines to show us how to find our way amid the broken sacred of the world.

But our tour guide is "the Preacher." As we have seen, when we ride his bus and look about, he takes up his loud-speaker and uses a voice that we do not expect. Now, as he points us to look out our windows and shows us what is out there, his method too will likely surprise us. After all, we entered this bus in order to enjoy a nice ride, learn a few things, and chitchat about life before and after lunch. We soon learn that our tour guide has little patience with small talk, has a lot on his mind, and seems quite troubled, even sad. He doesn't smile much. Far from creating a nice and cozy atmosphere, the first thing he does is to create tension for everyone on the bus.

Imagine two persons who work as tour guides of Poland. As you listen and see various sights, both guides give marvelous information regarding what is joyous and what is historically tragic as you travel through Warsaw or out to Auschwitz. But one guide possesses a qualitative difference from the other. This guide seems more melancholy, more deep-in-the-eyes when speaking. It feels as if there is something more to the tour for him than just the facts. During an afternoon break, you learn that this guide and his family lived through much of this history. The other guide does not have this heritage. The facts are the same, but the experience of those facts differs; and we who hear these two speak can feel it.

This analogy might help us as we try to understand the method the Preacher uses to tell us about what he sees. In the beginning, to call something "Eden," for example, was to identify it with everything pure, beautiful, and noble. God, people, animals, plants, space, and time all held hands and companioned together in true peace. All things inhabited the unharassed being of crimeless days beneath the glad provision of God. Because of this, every leaf, every piece of crumbled dirt, and every shining star that surrounded Eden shared this purposed and serene condition. To dwell "under the sun" was always and everywhere "Edenic." So, if any spokesperson for God would walk outside and have a look about, he would use two words to orient us guests or travelers to its geography. Life under the sun with all of its creatures and relations was "very good" (Gen. 1). Benediction (good words) saturated the place.

But that was the beginning of all things and a very long time ago. To enter the book of Ecclesiastes is to take a sobering tenth-century B.C.[2] tour of what once-Eden has now become. The "son of David" uses this book of Ecclesiastes to record what he sees for us when he steps outside "under the sun" and has a look at it all. He knows what it once was. He sees what it now is, and only one word in repetition will do. "Meaningless! Meaningless!" is his cry. To him, the place that was once called "very good" has disheveled into vanity. You see, for him to give us this tour, he must show us the now petalless rose. Nobility still exists. But it is a shell of its former self. An unexpected transparency rises.

AN UNEXPECTED LANGUAGE

It is not common for a king to set aside his credentials and take us into his confidence as if we both are only human, as if our humanity is the one true thing about us rather than the disparate positions and status that we separately hold. Consequently, the Preacher's language catches us off guard. Just as those who felt the water chase away the dirt on their feet could not imagine that it was Jesus who was kneeling to wash them, or just as those who felt it inappropriate that a king should have a stable for his birth or a donkey for his ride, so we too find it strange to hear this Preacher-king talk so humanly, so plainly.

First, his language is intimate. His manner of approach is first-person testimony. For example, he will tell us what his own thoughts and feelings have been as he looks at God, life, and himself. "I said in my heart," he reveals to us. "I applied my heart," he says.[3] It is rare for royalty or a person of position to speak so personally. Some of us are unaccustomed to or suspicious of someone who would teach us about God in such a subjective way.

But this spokesperson for God also leans toward poetic language.

All streams run to the sea,
    but the sea is not full;
to the place where the streams flow,
    there they will flow again. (Eccl. 1:7)

Those of us who are more steeped in the systematic language of Western theology may find instruction about God through poetic language unfamiliar and strange.

Proverbial language also flows from this son of David's lips.

It is better to go to the house of mourning
    than to go to the house of feasting,
for this is the end of all mankind,
    and the living will lay it to heart. (Eccl. 7:2)

Many of us desire more precision than the general truths a proverb conveys. We feel more at home with tidier sentiments in which what confounds us is solved. Lack of precision means that we have to enter the questions the proverb raises and leaves unanswered. "How is it better for us to spend time at the funeral parlor than at a house party with our friends?" "Is there a kind of instruction in either providence, and is one a better teacher than the other?" "Is he saying that being depressed is better in God's eyes than being happy?" A proverb intends us to question and wrestle.

Ecclesiastes will also confront us with the language of questions—and many without answers. "What does a man gain by all the toil by which he toils under the sun?" he asks, for example (Eccl. 1:3). In other words, "What it is the purpose of work, anyway?" Many of us have little capacity to do a day with unanswered questions. The spokesman for God calls us into this discomfort and wants us to see that God is there.

In all of this, his language unsettles us. As we have seen, not only does life have no meaning, this spokesman for God will describe the life God gives to each of us as an "unhappy business" (Eccl. 1:13). He will reveal to us that he "hated life" (Eccl. 2:17) and that some of us would have been better off had we never been born (Eccl. 6:3). Many of us might want to believe that such statements reveal an absence of faith. Our temptation is to quote a Bible verse or two and to resist the person saying such things. But Ecclesiastes will show us that such statements are made, in this case, on the basis of the fear of God.

Furthermore, the inductive approach of the book intentionally requires us to enter discomfort. What do I mean by that? The main point is not found until the end of the book. As a reader, you will have to start off with meaninglessness and wade through twelve chapters of tension, poetry, proverbs, unanswered questions, unsettling speech, and intimate language before arriving at the point he wants to make. Because of this approach, in order to get to the truth he wants us to see, we have to be willing to take a look at things we do not like. Show me a person who has no patience for encountering a story of sin and brokenness in a novel or a movie, and I will show you a person impatient with the people with whom they live. We have to be willing to walk and wade through the uncomfortable brokenness of life. Learning how to handle this book is an exercise itself, training us to wait and travel on amid the unanswered and everyday unpleasantness found in our real worlds. By taking up this method, the book intends to train us in our capacity for waiting upon God amid the uncomfortably unfixed. Lament surfaces on the bus as this guide tells us a story in such a way that tension grows and answers seemingly lessen.

A SACRED LAMENT

Some of us resist lament and therefore do not like this Preacher's method. For others of us, if we do lament, our tears are tantrums like the five-year-old who weeps and moans because she did not get the "Happy Meal" toy she wanted at McDonalds and is wounded because no one will satisfy her demand to get her a different toy. Some of us as adults still only know this kind of lament.

But Ecclesiastes is no tantrum. Nor is it the kind of lament that our addictions or idols stir up, like the loved one who wails because her bottle of bourbon, or gallon of ice cream, or damaging relationship, was removed from her. We cry not for ourselves in this case. We are lamenting the loss of something that wisdom would give thanks to be without. Ecclesiastes does not invite us to the lament of folly.

Instead, wisdom teaches us that tears, at their best, pay tribute to something lost that was once cherished and it was wise to cherish it. We lament the loss of a genuine good. This is why we ache when we look at the empty chair at our Christmas table and remember the one we loved who once sat there in tandem with us, but eats with us no more. The spokesman of Ecclesiastes likewise looks at what the created world has become. His language rises deep from an intense longing for what it was meant to be but is not. The lament is palpable.

> All his days are full of sorrow, and his work is a
>   vexation.
> Even in the night his heart does not rest. (Eccl. 2:23)

The curse of once-Eden remains. "In pain you shall eat of it . . . thorns and thistles it shall bring forth. . . . By the sweat of your face you shall eat bread" (Gen. 3:17–19).

What God created and purposed was legitimate and original good. To lose this good is pain. There are things worth crying about. To learn such tears for the Eden that once was is to learn how to cry like the wise we are meant to become.

A SACRED CYNICISM

This lament is likewise joined with cynicism, but not the kind found on the lips of one who is skeptical about God. Quite the contrary, you will find that the spokesman in Ecclesiastes is quite certain about God, his existence, his character, his mystery, and his goodness. Instead, the spokesman is cynical about the world and its creatures and promises.

No man has power to retain the spirit, or power over the day of death. There is no discharge from war, nor will wickedness deliver those who are given to it. All this I observed while applying my heart to all that is done under the sun, when man had power over man to his hurt. (Eccl. 8:8–9)

He doubts people, not God. But even here as he contemplates the powerlessness of people and the hurt that people cause one another, he is not cynical in a spoiled or academic way. He is not cynical in the manner of one who believes himself to know more among his books and late-night discussions than he does, and then tears his clothes over the state of the world among the pizza boxes of his well-paid-for dorm room.

Nor, as we will introduce more fully below, is he cynical about beauty or purpose the way many of us are. God "has made everything beautiful in its time" (Eccl. 3:11). A great many persons believe that "authenticity" means that we plumb the depths of the mire but we no longer recognize or speak freely about what is good in the world. Such "authenticity" struggles to remain authentic about goodness. The spokesman in Ecclesiastes has no such trouble. He still believes that beauty exists and that we are to cherish it. His ability to lament and express cynicism does not dampen his recognition of true goodness and joy. "I commend joy," he will declare (Eccl. 8:15)!

This is because the cynicism here is not leveled at the world itself. The king is not against trees or songs or food or love. Rather, his complaint has to do with the promise of "gain" that peddles its wares amid the rubble of once-Eden. For this reason, he will ask us as his readers a recurring question. "What does a man gain?"[4] After chronicling all of his enjoyment of music, drink, women, power over others, material possessions, land, and luxury he will conclude:

> I considered all that my hands had done and the toil
> I had expended in doing it, and behold, all was vanity and a striving after wind, and there was nothing
> to be gained under the sun. (Eccl. 2:11)

His question reveals that he has become cynical about what headway we can actually make when we strive to accumulate and take advantage of the offered pleasures in the world. For him, our attempts to use the money or drink or power or position or sex or fame to make ourselves happy and satisfied are foolhardy. There is no true gain from this use of the world.

My cousin told me that after his second tour as an American combat soldier in the war in Iraq, he only lasted five minutes the first time he went to a shopping mall upon his return from duty. This was a man, who like many others, found it hard to rest at home because of the nightly terrors from haunting combat memories that stalked his dreams. He was gradually finding rest again. I asked him further about the mall. He told me that he was filled with an intense anger at the heaps and heaps of stores and aisles and merchandise for sale being purchased. I asked him why. His answer has stuck with me and it might help you as you try to understand the point of view of the author of Ecclesiastes as he foreshadows Jesus. "After you've seen what the world is really like," he said, "it is hard to have patience with a mall."

The wise man of Ecclesiastes teaches us the same. As we begin to see what the world is really like, the things set before our eyes no longer satisfy us. The things sounding into our ears do not rest us. The reason is because every thing in once-Eden is sick. Even the most beautiful and good thing has a "weariness" within its bones (Eccl. 1:8).

Therefore, Ecclesiastes exposes us to this kind of lament, this kind of cynicism, so that we dull our taste for the trinkets of the world and learn to hunger instead for something truer, deeper, and richer.

To want more than is offered here under the sun, and then, on the basis of reverence for God, to scream for a new and different life: this well captures the vocal mood of this book.

A SACRED WORLDLINESS

But at this point, you will want to prepare yourself for a surprising twist. There is more than lament and cynicism awaiting you. Consider what I mean. I grew up singing a song that suggested that when we consider Jesus, the things of this earth will fade from view.[5]

Because there is no "gain" available to us in the world that can satisfy our soul hunger, we might think that therefore we are to find what satisfies us outside of the world. Finding God beyond the world, the things of the earth will therefore "grow strangely dim," and we will no longer concern ourselves with earthly things.

But you will discover that the writer of Ecclesiastes will not lead us to this "other-worldly" directive. His problem is not that we are seeking gain in the wrong place and therefore we need to leave the place in order to find what satisfies us. The place is not our problem. Our use of it is.

Consider a young person who every Friday night went out and found strangers to sexually "hook up" with. After a while, the physical contact and flirtation no longer satisfy. She feels empty. The kind of "gain" she is deriving from the caress of men is not satisfying her soul and its longings. She determines never to go out again on a Friday night. But the wise have learned that if she has not had some change in her soul, not going out again on a Friday will not answer her dilemma—after all there are six other days of the week and strange men willing for her touch each of those days. Friday nights, the gift of sex, and the company of friends are not in themselves wrong or evil. These earthly things are not the problem—what we try to do with them is. She is trying to use them for a gain that they cannot and were never intended to provide.

Consequently, the things of earth will grow strangely dim in the sense of the "gain" they offer us in comparison to the satisfaction of soul provided for by the One who created and redeemed us. But in terms of their own worth and value in his hands, as we see the Lord, we will actually begin to see the things of the earth more brilliantly in their proper light. Therefore, like our Savior who taught us that we are meant to behold the character of God as we look upon the birds of the air or the lilies of the fields, so the writer of Ecclesiastes will tell us that "light is sweet, and it is pleasant for the eyes to see the sun" (Eccl. 11:7).

This then is the surprise! Learning a sacred lament and cynicism will not forbid us from finding pleasure in seeing the sun even while meaninglessness bustles about beneath it. Even more surprising is that the "gain" we are meant to have and that we all long for will come from God now, in much the same fashion as it did for Adam and

32

Eve in Eden. Like them, we will learn by grace not to use the place to find the gain we truly require. But like them, neither will that gain come by trying to escape once-Eden or God. Rather, we will learn gain in God among the ordinary joys of his giving.

A SACRED JOY

The result of this sacred worldliness is the discovery and recovery of true joy (true gain). With God, even amid the meaninglessness, the madness, the lament, and the cynicism, a human being "will not much remember the days of his life because God keeps him occupied with joy in his heart" (Eccl. 5:20).

So, when the Westminster Shorter Catechism instructs us that our purpose in life is to glorify and enjoy God forever, it is as if the book of Ecclesiastes asks the question: "*Where* do we glorify and enjoy God forever?" The answer is: "Right here where you are under the sun."

Then it raises and answers another question: "*How* do we glorify and enjoy God right where we are? For where we are is filled with meaninglessness, madness, and empty pleasures." It will answer: "By recovering Eden and learning to find true gain in the 'withness' of God" among ordinary things.

For this reason, we will learn to think it sad and empty to see or become a person who has everything but has no "power" from God "to enjoy them" and therefore whose "soul is not satisfied with life's good things" (Eccl. 6:2–3). We will learn to believe that "there is nothing better" than to have a place to inhabit, a thing to do in that place, and some people in that place to share it with. With God, such small things are happy and gainful. We taste again what Adam and Eve once felt in Eden before they lost their thirst for the sacred mundane and made a wreck of it all.

ONE GREATER THAN SOLOMON

And now, consider one last remark by way of our introduction. As we read Ecclesiastes together, and enter the "wreck of it all," we will be led time and again from Ecclesiastes to Jesus Christ. It is Jesus, after all, who is the true King and the true Son of David that Solomon foreshadows. One "greater than Solomon is here," Jesus proclaimed (Matt. 12:42). In Solomon, we see a foretaste of the true Sage, Jesus. Therefore, the language, teachings, footsteps, cross, and resurrection of Jesus will inform our reading.

Consider the language of our Lord Jesus. He speaks with intimacy, lament, poetry, proverbs, and questions. With sacred cynicism, he too will interrogate our ideas of "gain" and loss. "For what does it profit a man to gain the whole world and forfeit his soul?" Jesus will ask (Mark 8:36).

The Savior, likewise, will also sift through the offer made by the world's provisions. The earth's treasures can be beautiful, but they are of the kind which rust or moth can consume and eat away, he will tell us. They are like valuables made breakable by thieves and sold off for a bribe. We will require a treasure of a different kind, Jesus will say. We need a kind of gain, a treasure that has heaven in it and is able to remain intact though rust and moth and thief do their worst (Matt. 6:19–20).

Similarly, there is a kind of water, Jesus teaches us, that though we drink it over and over again, it cannot satisfy us. By "water" Jesus meant, in the first place, the misuse of sex and relationships. A woman was drinking that kind of water repeatedly but was still broken and empty. Jesus counseled her that there was a different kind of water that if she drank from it her thirst would be satisfied and her taste for other waters would diminish. By this "different kind of water" Jesus meant himself (see John 4). Only God himself can satisfy our thirsting souls. Without his provision and empowerment we can have "everything" and nothing.

There is something of this sacred worldliness that likewise surfaces in Jesus' prayer for his followers. "I do not ask that you take them out of the world," Jesus prayed, "but that you keep them from the evil one" (John 17:15). How is it that we embrace where we are without trying to make it do what only God can do for us? How do we forsake the "gain" the world offers while remaining engaged with the good that God has given in the world?

Likewise, the footsteps or "ways" that Jesus lived resembles the God who wants us to navigate life with the language that can handle it. For a moment we remind ourselves of the Gospels and what we see and hear in them of Jesus. Is Jesus sappy, sentimental, and naive, when he talks about loving enemies and the chronically ill? His poetic language and parables are dressed with the earthy and down-home. Jesus take us into all the spooky hallways and messes of life, and teaches his disciples to follow him there. And doesn't this Son of God go to the cross, the place of injustice and cruelty, where death seems meaningless and pleasures cannot satisfy, and from there he says, "It is fulfilled"? Christ is the gain that the world cannot provide. His is the redemption that causes flowers blooming to find notice again.

Just as Adam and Eve were given a place and food and work and each other within which God would walk with them and satisfy their souls, so this pattern remains for us. God intends to be found amid our toast and coffee, while we swing a hammer or change a diaper. This is why he is called "Immanuel." It means "God is with us." God is with us here with our tennis shoes and hair spray and hospital beds. This is the promise Jesus made. While his disciples cleaned fish or told jokes with each other or testified or wrongly suffered, he would not remove them from such things, but rather he would "be with" them always in the midst (Matt. 28:20).

We will learn that this Jesus not only saves us but becomes our wisdom. Jesus purchases that wisdom for us. Like the original audience of Ecclesiastes, we too are not meant to live as a naive people. Those of us who ostrich our heads in the sand, he will lift us up to the ground. It is time to cry then at what we see. It is time to laugh at what is worthy of our laughter. In Jesus, the true Solomon and Son of David, we learn as his people to become the tour guides and mall maps of the world. "Here is where you are," we say by grace to those around us. "Here is what things once were like and here is what it is like in the world now and here is the language you need to wisely get through it with God." This is what we were meant for. Wherever "there" is, we have God-given language for it. It is a voice and a language that we never expected God to give us. But he did.

THE UNEXPECTED GOD

Now what does this mean for those who believe the Bible to be God's Word? Because we submit to the inspiration and inerrancy of this book, we are meant, along with the original audience of God's people, to receive this unexpected voice and language as coming from God himself. We are meant to ask ourselves a question such as: "What does it tell me about God that he wants us to hear that everything is meaningless or that he recognizes our sometimes hatred of life?"

To receive his voice in this book is to learn that God is not afraid to use language that is personal, poetic, and proverbial, filled with unanswered questions and saturated with unsettling statements, to reveal himself. It also seems that we are meant to see that God is quite willing to invite us into a book and a life in which we walk toward the end without everything being fixed, answered, or settled before we get there.

This means that God can "go there." But because of the safe, clean-cut, pristine, sentimental, or naive approaches to

Christianity and church that have mentored many of us, we may cherish a mistaken notion that God resembles a more G-rated approach to life. Ecclesiastes reminds us, however, that wherever *there* is, whatever the conversation, whatever the question or unsettling situation, God is able and willing to go there. There is a kind of authenticity that God is willing to set before us in this book that would make many of us who pride ourselves on transparency clam up. It is as if God plays the "you think that's bad" game with us. To whatever we say, he says, "You think that's bad? Let me tell you something more." Ecclesiastes seems like one of God's ways to say to us, This world and your life are more broken than you now realize and what God created for us is more satisfying than we believe. Like Adam and Eve, we too still strive for things out there and damage ourselves in the process all the while God's gift and presence were right in front of us.

God shows us in other books and in Jesus that he is the Redeemer, the Savior from our sins. But here, God shows us also that he is our Creator, the satisfier of our human hearts, the namer of what is broken, the wisdom for our lives. As his people, we are not only supposed to get our future taken care of by relating to God through Christ, we are also meant to learn how to navigate the fallen, broken, beautiful world as human beings with the remaining gift and witness that is ours as his creatures. Until God's people become savvy with the world according to his wisdom, we will be a naive, gullible, romanticizing, and sentimental people. God wants his people *wise* toward what is there.

Likewise, he intends to teach us what it can mean for us to gain a stamina for learning slowly and uncomfortably. Instead of stopping someone who tells us that they hate life, maybe we are supposed to listen to the unanswered moment and enter the discomfort with the language or silence that God gives us. Maybe we are meant to ask, "What is it about things under the sun that makes this person of God say he hates life?" Perhaps we are meant as God's people to learn how to enter such things with him.

After all, he is already there in the midst. Most of us would not anticipate that kind of voice from this kind of person. But by exposing us to this disorientation, God is preparing us to wisely do life in a fallen world. Job's friends, like us, often struggle here. Therefore, God seems to believe that if we are to learn how to wisely do life, then our systematic categories, answers to every question, tidy explanations, formal language, deductive assumptions, and a resistance to what is subjective will not prove adequate for us.

To make this personal, my half sister died as a young teenager. She was diagnosed as having a Pnet Sarcoma. The clinical diagnosis helped identify the dark thing. It gave us a name for the cause of the nightmare. But the clinical language could not describe the experience of the nightmare. Nor could it provide language suitable for getting through it. A different kind of language was needed by the graveside.

There weren't many flowers by your casket.
You didn't want them, remember?
Flowers seemed too old and you were too young
    for this.
We all were.
What you wanted was balloons:
colors and shapes and printed sayings,
bundled air on dangling strings made for temporary
    use.
Your body lay empty while they danced on the wind
    and we cried.
Shovels leaned against an old Chevy truck, parked
    at a distance.
Dirt piles hidden for the purpose.
Black scarves and a yellow rose; the hands of strangers
with dust in their fingernails.
They waited for the lowering to begin.
I longed for the lowering to wait.
These balloons of yours, bumping and thumping
    in the wind,

a nagging intrusion of sights and sounds.
What were they doing here? Distractions
to my attention.
I smudged my cheeks with fingertips and tears.
The balloons bumped and pulled at what held them.
With upwards bursts and jolts they seemed restless
     to fly
untied from these rented poles of aluminum,
holding tarp above your grave.
Then I let go of my rose and set it down, balloons
     making their escape.
That's when I said it. "Sometimes a Styrofoam cup
     can hold the ocean."
I just wanted you to know that it was you who taught
     me that.

God intends to reveal himself as the One Who Goes There. He intends to equip his people with a voice and language and method that has the capacity to do the same. "Getting prepared by God to find a language adequate for handling life as it is": this is the calling set before us in Ecclesiastes. This is the kind of discipleship offered by the sage to his student. This is the kind of apologetic that the Preacher invites those who listen into. This is the kind of evangelistic hint this pastor uses to see his hearers converted to God.

AN UNEXPECTED PASTORAL APOLOGETIC

In short, the voice and method of this Preacher apprentices us in a sage way of talking with others about God. This approach emphasizes the following assumptions:

- *God as Creator*: We learn from the Preacher to start with God, not just as our soulish Redeemer, but as our Creator and as the one who governs the seasons and circumstances of our physical reality.

39

- *Human*: We set aside our credentials as those who follow God and humbly remember that we too are human beings along with others. We are creaturely. We do not require knowledge of redemptive history in order to have a conversation. Nor do we pretend that we ourselves do not question, feel, think, or misfire.
- *Inductive*: We recognize that sometimes the answers only come later after one has wrestled and searched. This takes time. We learn to wait amid unanswered questions and confused moments. Our solution to tension resists quick fixes, trite answers, or tantrums.
- *Hospitable*: We become hospitable toward negative thoughts and emotions. We resist minimizing and exaggerating things in order to make them what we want them to be. Instead, we learn to receive things as they are and to believe that God will have something to say and do about things as they are. We become hospitable rather than hostile toward the questions that our fellow human beings and we raise under the sun.
- *Poetic*: We learn the language of poetry, riddle, and proverb. Alongside other kinds of didactic language found in the Bible, we recognize the value of this kind of unsettling and less tidy language for our walk with God and each other.
- *Local*: We begin to recover a sense of God's provision for our joy in the ordinary. Instead of always looking elsewhere, we begin to learn that God meets us in the local work, relationships, food, and place that he has given to us.

As we hear this Preacher talk to us in this God-centered, human, inductive, hospitable, poetic, and local way, we begin to see a foreshadowed picture of how God himself has graciously related to each one of us. He has centered himself in our lives, not just as our Redeemer, but also as the one who created us and the one who governs all of our seasons. He is the one who recovers our humanity and delivers us from acting as if we or others are God. He is the one who humbled himself humanly on our behalf in Jesus. He has not required that we know everything up front or that we have all the answers or that we cannot question, make mistakes, or need to grow. Rather, he has been hospitable toward all of our aches, questions, sins, laments, frustrations, and wrestlings with the way things are. He has given us room and taken a long perseverance with us to bring us where we are in him. He has not been squeamish with us to make things simpler than they are or to leave us void of language which is able to meet us in our pain. Nor has he been arrogant or dismissive toward the small things that are meaningful to us. In fact, it is here in our mundane work, prayer, relationships, food, and life that God has been with us. In Jesus, God has come to us in these very ways so that he might empathize with us and look honestly with us at the state of things, in order to disciple us, reason with us, win us to himself, and all of this by his earthy grace.

CONCLUSION

The poetry that began this chapter pictures a farmer facing what he would rather not but must. The "long winter nights" of frozen fields and dead ground cause him to adjust his dreams but not to resign them. And this, it seems to me, matters very much. For many stop dreaming amid the cloud-covered fields of their lives.

> He who observes the wind will not sow,
>   and he who regards the clouds will
>   not reap. (Eccl. 11:4)

He is no romantic. His "dreams are narrow" amid the cold. But he dreams nonetheless because God has not left us to warm ourselves by some other fire.

41

> As you do not know the way the spirit comes to the bones in the womb of a woman with child, so you do not know the work of God who makes everything. In the morning sow your seed, and at evening withhold not your hand, for you do not know which will prosper, this or that, or whether both alike will be good. (Eccl. 11:5–6)

His is a bone-frigid dream born from putting his booted feet into the same old once-fruitful dirt and dreaming of the roots it could once more sustain. A song begins to sound from his humming lips blue in the cold with breath like smoke rising in the morning air of winter. He gives his life to a repetition of planting and plowing amid the cold ordinary. "Over and over he enters the furrow."

After all, amid the madness, who knows what God might do?

QUESTIONS FOR DISCUSSION

1. How is Ecclesiastes like a park ranger?
2. What about the Preacher's use of language makes you uncomfortable? Encourages you?
3. What does Ecclesiastes teach us about lament? How is this kind of lament different from what you are used to?
4. Describe the cynicism of Ecclesiastes? How does it differ from other forms of cynicism?
5. What does Ecclesiastes teach us about joy? Do you find this kind of joy appealing?
6. Look at the pastoral apologetic. Which aspects of this apologetic challenge you? Help you?
7. How does the book of Ecclesiastes point us to the person and work of Jesus?

CHAPTER THREE

FINDING GAIN

The roadside flowers, too wet for the bee,
Expend their bloom in vain.[1]

In Frank Capra's classic film *It's a Wonderful Life*, George Bailey struggles to believe that his hometown of Bedford Falls possesses enough within it to sustain him. He seizes dreams, and those dreams suggest that Bedford Falls is too overlooked to provide the life of wonder he desires. Therefore, the idea of living in an old house, with one woman in long love, in a little place, with the same old job, the same old enemies, and seeking there the good of those local neighbors, causes George Bailey to fidget with the mundane, restless to leave it behind him. He wants to gain more for his life. "I couldn't face being cooped up for the rest of my life in a shabby little office," he declares to his pop. "I want to do something big, something important."

This story has endured for so many years, because at least two assumptions live within George's thoughts that we too recognize within our own.

One, George assumes that if importance is to be gained in this life, he must travel to a patch of earth somewhere other than where he presently resides in order to find it.

Two, he believes that once he finds it, he will become a satisfied and happy man, content, experienced, honored, and fulfilled; no longer restless within himself or the world.

If these two ideas in George's head are balloons, then Ecclesiastes 1 is a needle meant to pop them. Or maybe closer to the matter, if these two assumptions are like the street performer's illusions drawing a crowd toward the corners of our minds, then Ecclesiastes 1 is the masked foil that risks his reputation to reveal the secrets behind the magician's tricks.

The needle, the masked revealer of this sleight of hand, comes in the form of a penetrating question. The Preacher asks, "What does man gain by all the toil at which he toils under the sun?" (Eccl. 1:3).

On the one hand, the word *gain* likely carries the linguistic idea of "making a profit." In the war-torn world, seasons of peace give us hope that after we finish our dinner we will retain a surplus to put in the fridge—leftovers fit for rewarming and tomorrow's lunch. We hope that after paying taxes and meeting our monthly needs, we will garner enough savings to accumulate in a sock under our bed or in an account in our bank.

But on the other hand, the Preacher places this word *gain* within the context of his search for what is humanly meaningful with what is not (Eccl. 1:2). By doing so, he gives us a strong hint that he intends us to assess "gain" more broadly than our material holdings. Not only are we a materially famished people working and thieving about, earners and hoarders of coin and cloth; but we are likewise a soul-starved people, scavenging for emotional and rational leftovers, searching for a reason, a purpose, a point to it all; attempting finally to arrive. We want our lives to count!

Because we are prone to take this material and soul search for significance to the earth, the Preacher painfully deconstructs these dreams. He baldly declares that whether we remain here or go there in the earth, the issue for us remains harshly the same. There exists no place or thing "under the sun," that can separate the stowaway drudgery that attends all of our earthly doings (toil).

Looking "under the sun" for "gain" by our "toil" is like trying to buy medicine in a shoe store. The shoe store really matters, but no medicine is found there. So it is in the earth. Whether we move or stay, spend or save, nothing and no one can make our lives pay off or yield the return for which we hope. For all of its beauty and dignity, the earth simply does not possess this ability.

We refuse to believe this. So, the Preacher uses the rest of this chapter to prove the point.

INTRODUCTIONS

When I was in school, I was taught that an essay or talk had three main components: (1) an introduction, (2) a body, and (3) a conclusion. In the introduction, I was taught that we say what we intend to say. In the body we say it. In the conclusion, we remind everyone of what we just said.

As you read Ecclesiastes 1 it might help you to recognize that it serves as an introduction to the book as a whole. In chapter 1, the Preacher briefly prepares us for the subjects and themes that he intends to talk about once he begins chapter 2.

I was also taught that a talk or an essay usually centers around one main theme or one big idea that the listener or reader is meant to grapple with. An old adage for preachers says that "a mist in the pulpit creates a fog in the pew." If we do not understand what we are trying to say, it is likely true that those listening will get lost in the windy condensation of our leaf-blown words.

The main thing that this Preacher wants us to grapple with goes something like this:

What? Everything is meaningless.
Why? Because the gain we seek does not exist under
    the sun.

In this light, how are we to understand what the Preacher means when he repeatedly says "everything is vanity" or "meaningless"?

To begin, remember that by "everything," the Preacher refers to what is "under the sun," here in the created world. What the Preacher calls "under the sun" was once Edenic, with its perfect creation and painless providences. Now all that is under heaven remains only a cursed shell of its former self—sad and needing recovery.

Then, reflect with me for a moment on how language is used. For example, the neighbor who says, "There is no absolute truth," makes an absolute truth claim. The neighbor wants us to believe that it is true that no truth exists. Likewise, the neighbor who says that "language is nonsense" intends us to make sense of her language. She hopes that we will think and act as if it makes sense to us that her words are nonsense.

Similarly, the neighbor who says that "love is an illusion: nothing more than a chemical reaction in our brains" will nonetheless weep at the loss of a pet; lose hair, weight, and sleep when his spouse has an affair; worry about their children on the first day of school; and cry with ache at the graveside of a friend.

When we speak against truth, meaning, or love, we are necessarily contradictory. We are like the woman who uses a blog to decry social media or the man who uses a pen, paper, typewriter, or computer to address the evils of technology. Without social media the woman couldn't decry it. Without technology the man couldn't write against it. So it is with truth and meaning. The only way for a human being to disregard truth and meaning is to appeal to both. To speak against them we must uphold them.

So, when the Preacher opens his book by saying that everything is meaningless, it will help us to remember that he makes a statement that is actually quite full of meaning. When he declares that "all is vanity," he presumes to have stated a truth that is not in vain. The difference between him and the skeptic is that he knows he is contradictory. In fact, he hopes that those reading or listening to him will actually take seriously what he is saying, will find meaning from it, and will thereby discover what is true about the way things are "under the sun." Ultimately, the Preacher wants to point out what is vain in order for us to discover what isn't.

OUR TIMES FADE FROM MEMORY

To begin, the Preacher wants us to remember that, under the sun, "a generation goes, and a generation comes" (Eccl. 1:4). A "generation" refers to the cycle of persons and providences that exist in the world. To picture the meaning of this, take a moment and draw a straight line on a piece of paper. At the front of that drawn line write, "my birth." At the back of that drawn line write, "my death." The short line between "my birth" and "my death" represents my years, my generation. Several of these lines with births and deaths chain-linked together create a picture of one generation that surfaces as another one fades. Our lives along with those with whom we grow up, and the circumstances that formed our nightly news, are but a short breath, drawn in and let out.

The Hebrew poet soberly captures the sense.

The years of our life are seventy,
or even by reason of strength eighty;
yet their span is but toil and trouble;
they are soon gone, and we fly away. (Ps. 90:10)

People are soon forgotten. As I write, a national discussion recently arose from the Grammy Awards, which annually honors those who participate in the music industry. Sir Paul McCartney performed live on stage. In response, a large population of young people posed the question,

"Who is Paul McCartney?" (Perhaps you too are asking that question?) Famously, a similar happening once took place when a student excitedly told Eugene Peterson, "Dr. Peterson, Bono quoted you!" In response, Peterson said, "That's wonderful! Who is Bono?" Some of us reading have heard of neither.

Less famously, imagine you attended a youth gathering with me in which the question was asked, "Who was George Jetson's dog?"

Mention Joe DiMaggio, Shirley Temple, Dizzy Gillespie, Johnny Carson, or *Butch Cassidy and the Sundance Kid* and young persons say, "Who?" Mention Albert Pujols, Carly Shay, Ryan Tedder, Jimmy Fallon, or *Twilight* and the elderly say, "What?"

When I was a boy, an "oldies station" played music on the radio from the 1950s. Now that I am a man, "oldies stations" include music from the 1980s when I was in high school and college.

This coming and going can haunt us. Even the great works of Joseph in Egypt fade. "Now there arose a new king over Egypt, who did not know Joseph" (Ex. 1:8). Even Moses and Joshua and all the remarkable happenings of God disappear. "There arose another generation after them who did not know the LORD or the work that he had done for Israel" (Judg. 2:10).

There is no remembrance of former things,
    nor will there be any remembrance
of later things yet to be
    among those who come after. (Eccl. 1:11)

If we stop and think about it, we have never heard of almost everyone who has ever lived. Most of those we have heard of we do not personally know. Even those few who go down in history, whom some of us thoroughly study in pursuit of advanced degrees, remain incompletely remembered.

I attended a school orientation for my daughter. The junior high teachers reminded us that the young people now entering junior high do not know from personal experience what "September 11" means. Only eleven years later, an event that profoundly changed the lives of a generation becomes a chapter in a history book summarized for bored seventh graders, studying for a quiz. Whatever we clutch, tarnish, collect, or strive for will soon enough fade from memory. Where is the gain in that?

The Preacher then adds an observation from nature for emphasis. A generation comes. A generation goes, *"but the earth remains forever."* The "sun," the "wind," the "streams," and "the sea" of the earth will all outlast our individual human life spans (Eccl. 1:5–7). The hyperbole of "forever" emphasizes how deeply contrasted are the length of years in which a human being lives with the length of years that the sun rises and sets. Look at the sun as it shines, and the Preacher's point is made. For we view today the same sun that Adam and Eve saw. Or consider the river Jordan. It is spoken of from the book of Genesis throughout the Bible. The Jordan has outlasted the earthly sojourns of Abraham, Moses, Joshua, David, Elisha, John the Baptist, the apostles, and our Lord Jesus. The river Jordan watched me as well, as I stood by it in 2003, and then I too left.

The Preacher's point is this: When we die, the sun will rise the next morning, the waters will tide, and the wind will blow, while other human beings after us will likewise come, take their turn, and go. So, our worst and best days fade. Our celebrations and our tragedies disappear. Perhaps it comforts us to know that loss will not last. But it aches to embrace a waning joy.

For this reason, looking for gain in what exists outside of our windows during the days of our lives is like trying to make a snowman endure in Indiana. The winter fades. The yard thaws. Spring and summer have their way. Generations are like Missouri leaves. They bloom in spring but then fall for the raking. Toiling among fading peoples and times, in order to try and make our lives count, is fruitless.

EVERYTHING IS TIRED

Because the earth has this sense of permanence to it, some are tempted therefore to lift their eyes off of humanity and onto the sun, wind, or seas as the source of gain for their lives.

There is no denying the soothing pleasure of nature. "Light is sweet, and it is pleasant for the eyes to see the sun" (Eccl. 11:7). When I was a boy, I listened to a popular song and gladly sang along. The song described how the sunshine can brighten not only our days but our hearts and minds.[2]

But when one catches a prominent entertainer offstage at home behind closed doors without the lights and the makeup, sometimes the view surprises: the face worn from travel, the thoughts fatigued from constant producing; the unhappy sense that for all the attention and thrilling moments, something still remains missing within. Similarly, the Preacher peels back the curtain of creation and lets us peek into its window. He shows us that offstage, even vibrant nature is more discontented by the monotony of nonstop performances than she appears.

All streams run to the sea,
    but the sea is not full;
to the place where the streams flow,
    there they flow again. (Eccl. 1:7)

Flowing and flowing, always back to the same old place, but never full and always without rest.

In Greek mythology, Sisyphus is a man condemned to repeat the same meaningless task over and again without end. He rolls a boulder up a mountain only to watch it

50

roll down again. Rolling the boulder, watching it fall, and pushing it up again describes his endless days with no relief.

The Preacher has said as much regarding the sun, the streams, and the wind. "Under the sun," we sweat with heat and squint from the shine. So does the earth beneath it. It is like Sisyphus. For this reason, the Preacher tells us in Ecclesiastes 1:8, "All things are full of weariness." Everything of man, toil, earth, sun, wind, and sea is tired.

Where I come from, we call it "bone tired." One is so worn out that the bones ache. This kind of fatigue goes beyond words. The Preacher implies for us that all creation is bone tired. "A man cannot utter it," he says (Eccl. 1:8). The weary mumble into bed with their shoes still on.

The apostle Paul will take up the cause of this exhausted and unsatisfied realm of once-Eden with its beleaguered persons, plants, animals, and waters. Paul will take it up with poetry too. He will write that creation is like a slave, "subjected to futility," in "bondage to corruption" longing to be "set free." She is like a woman pained in childbirth. Once-Eden has become a place that groans (Rom. 8:20–23).

It is little wonder then, that God in his wisdom and kindness has urged us not to set our clutching hopes for gain on the groaning things.

> Beware lest you raise your eyes to heaven, and when you see the sun and the moon and the stars, all the host of heaven, you be drawn away and bow down to them and serve them, things that the LORD your God has allotted to all the peoples under the whole heaven. (Deut. 4:19)

Creation too is like a shoe store for someone needing medicine. It can provide something good for us, but it cannot satisfy our true need. This is why our efforts with people or nature to accumulate an abiding surplus for our bodies and souls elude us.

> The eye is not satisfied with seeing,
> nor the ear filled with hearing. (Eccl. 1:8)

Nothing that we see or hear under the sun can bring us the gain for which we strive. Sunshine is pleasant and happy. But it cannot satisfy us. Everything we sense leaves us restless. Like a child two days after Christmas, or lovers two days after holding hands for the first time, we grow bored even with good things. We always want more.

EVERYTHING IS OLD

And all of this is old news. According to the Preacher, this is nothing but the same old story of every human being in every time and place.

> What has been is what will be . . .
> and there is nothing new under the sun.
> Is there a thing of which it is said,
> "See this is new"?
> It has been already
> in the ages before us. (Eccl. 1:9–10)

When the Preacher makes his case that everything new is an old thing repeated, he does not refer to technology and invention in its various forms. If we were to speak to him today, he would readily acknowledge that gummy bear vitamins, Super Bowl commercials, a space station, laser technology, and Nike® shoes did not exist in his time and are new inventions. The things people create are not his focus.

Rather, the context of this chapter makes clear that his focus references the toil of human beings under the sun and the absence of gain that it provides them. As it relates to the seasons, conditions, temptations, and longings associated with being human, nothing new takes place that hasn't already confronted those who have gone before us.

Every human being has tried to navigate food, clothing, and shelter. Each one has wrestled with what it means to work, to provide a way of life, to make their way, to hope and weep for their children. Crimes, wounds, and enemies are not new. Handling weather patterns, sickness, romance, aging, sadness, forgiveness, commitment, laughter, and dreams has not originated with us. Putting a space station in the skies has not kept our families intact, delivered us from dictators, or eradicated a selfish heart. New inventions make our bones heal quicker but not our minds, not our hearts.

When I was a teenager, the rock band Foreigner helped me to ask what love is.[3] I sang it too, right along with them, with all of my adolescent heart. Neither the Preacher nor many of us reading will have ever heard of Foreigner, their music, or the band members' names. But every human being, no matter what the time, place, or language of their generation, has grappled with this question of love, has made its mistakes and felt its joys and pains, withstood regimes of hatred, desired for themselves and their children to know its meaning.

A young one in love is an ancient thing. Spring rains are old-fashioned. Most human questions have hung around. Death speaks all languages. Uniqueness does not bring about the gain for which we strive. After all, the next new thing is a hand-me-down.

WE ARE PERSONALLY LIMITED

At this point, the Preacher places his own personal story into this long and toilsome march of persons, nature, and repeated history. Like each of us, he too takes a part in this drawn-out drama.

Whether this is Solomon himself or one playing the part of Solomon as some scholars suggest, rarely in history (if ever) does the king of a nation present himself so humbly and transparently. Even modern-day CEOs, politicians, coaches, or pastors normally resist this kind of authentic candor.

Furthermore, his is no isolationist policy, no escapist religion. He is discontent with second-hand knowledge. He chooses not to remove himself from the tangled world but rather to enter it by means of wisdom and to sort it out. He has kept his eyes and ears open to the news. He has neither dismissed nor mocked madness. Instead, he has tried responsibly to listen to, learn about, and make an accounting of "all that is done," whether insane or otherwise, beneath the muggy glare of it all.

> I the Preacher have been king over Israel in Jerusalem. And I applied my heart to seek and to search out by wisdom all that is done under heaven. (Eccl. 1:12–13)

Because of this humble posture, some might overlook this king. But we needn't let the transparency fool us. The king of Israel in Jerusalem at that time was nothing less than the anointed king of the people of God. As king, he makes clear for us that he is not everywhere at once, and that he is not the ruler of all things. He resides in a local place (Israel, Jerusalem). He also admits that he does not know everything. He too has had to resist hardheaded folly and to take up the humbled posture required of anyone who wants to learn (to seek, to search). Like any other human being he has his own interior life (heart), and he too must dependently lean, and be teachable, toward what wisdom requires.

> Yes, if you call out for insight
>   and raise your voice for understanding,
> *if you seek it like silver*
>   *and search for it as for hidden treasures,*
> then you will understand the fear of the LORD
>   and find the knowledge of God. (Prov. 2:3–5)

Similarly, when he says that no one in Jerusalem before him has ever had the wisdom and experience that he possesses (Eccl. 1:16), we might think it nothing but the grand boastings of a small man, the ramblings of a big fish in a little pond, until we remember that the one who came before him was David, a mighty king remembered still among the stories of nations.

We also might want to dismiss the Preacher's claim to "have seen *everything* that is done under the sun" (Eccl. 1:14). What can a local man know about all that is done in the world?

Yet, we know that global savvy can be greatly gained by paying close local attention to what most overlook. For what takes place out there "under heaven" also shows up here, within our own country and within our own towns. As king, he also interacts with representatives from across the globe (1 Kings 10:1ff).

"Applying his heart," therefore, he has gained the perspective of wise experience. It is from this experience that the Preacher will use the rest of this book to list out all of the ways that we vainly try to toil for gain among persons and places that cannot provide it. He is a sage guide and we are wise to learn from him. So, why does he take up this humbly transparent posture?

His power and his knowledge, like that of everyone else, is limited.

> What is crooked cannot be made straight,
>> and what is lacking cannot be counted.
>> (Eccl. 1:15)

His happiness under the sun cannot find its compliment.

> For in much wisdom is much vexation,
>> and he who increases knowledge increases
>> sorrow. (Eccl. 1:18)

He tells us that he too, for all of his power, position, and advantages, is like a man who runs around in his yard trying to catch wind in his hands (Eccl. 1:17). Though a king, as he applies his heart to life, he too remains like one who keeps plunging his arms into the air and grasping at nothing whatsoever.

No matter how called or wise he is, no matter how helpful and necessary his mentoring will prove to be for us, even a man of God still squints and sweats beneath the sun. To use even a man of God to accrue gain under the sun is a vanity. After all, Solomon died. So will we. Even the very wise cannot fix the world.

OUR UNHAPPY BUSINESS

So, at this moment, if we have followed Jesus for any amount of time, we might feel profoundly ready for the Preacher to now make an evangelistic turn. Though we have only covered the introduction to his "sermon," the Preacher has already dismantled the earthly persons and things that we are prone to clutch or stomp in order to try and make our lives count. We might feel that surely it is time now for the Preacher to tell us about God. For the Preacher's message about our toiling for gain among things that cannot provide it sounds so much like what Jesus will tell us.

> Do not lay up for yourselves treasures on earth, where moth and rust destroy and where thieves break in and steal, but lay up for yourselves treasures in heaven, where neither moth nor rust destroys and where thieves do not break in and steal. For where your treasure is, there your heart will be also. (Matt. 6:19–21)

> Do not work for the food that perishes, but for the food that endures to eternal life. (John 6:27)

The Preacher will tell us about God, but not in the manner that we may expect.

This Preacher is no quick healer. In his evangelism, he has taken the posture, not of the sermonizer, but of the pained and skeptical human being, the raw searcher who wants an honest word with no spin about the way things really are. This evangelistic process, if it is one, is a slow one, therefore. Weekend sermons beneath a rented tent will not do. Having integrity regarding what one sees in the world requires honest questions. True questioners will not trifle with quick slogans and slanted banners. Answering wisely takes time. Taking time amid things not yet answered provokes discomfort—a discomfort often required in order to recover spiritual health. A sickly child grimaces to swallow the dark liquid that will recover her smile.

So, the Preacher tells us about God, but not as our Redeemer; not yet. At this moment we are meant to consider God as the one who governs and has authority over that which is under the sun. God is the one who lets the gainless world go on as it is. God is the one who does not stop our having to deal with vanity. For this reason, it can feel that God is like the nameless substitute teacher who gives busywork to fidgety students. We must face this fact.

> It is an unhappy business that God has given to the children of man to be busy with. (Eccl. 1:13)

May I suggest that at this point we are like those who read Jane Austen's famed novel *Pride and Prejudice*? We are introduced to "Mr. Darcy" as a dark and brooding figure. By fits and starts his distant and frowning posture leads us to think all manner of distasteful things owing to his obviously disreputable character. But time reveals our error. Like those characters in the story, we too gravely mistake Mr. Darcy's furrowed brows to represent something other than the truly noble character he actually possesses.

Likewise, it is almost as if the Preacher has taken a snapshot of that frowning moment in the garden of Eden. As Adam and Eve fig-leaf themselves with shame and the Serpent is silent and caught in his treason, God declares a curse upon all that he had made. They will live. But from that point on, thorns, thistles, pain, and sweat await them all "east" of Eden (Gen. 3:14–24).

The Preacher does exalt God. But what he exalts is that aspect of God's character which did not relieve Adam, Eve, or the Serpent from sin's consequences. We see his brooding and frowning. This is the God who governs us. He did not stop the unhappy business of paradise lost. We must linger here.

This part of God's story tells us that God will not bring salvation by giving us escape and immunity from the now-cursed world. Jesus too will highlight this lack of escape throughout his teachings. "In the world, you will have tribulation," he assures us (John 16:33).

We will have to come to terms with this fact about God. If there is no escape from what is under the sun, then rescue will have to come from somewhere else. The time will come in which God will personally squint and sweat beneath the sun's light and heat. He will enter the gainless world, endure its vanity, and feel the pain of it. "In the world, you will have tribulation," Jesus will one day say. "The poor you will always have with you," he will declare. In that, he will sound just like Solomon in Ecclesiastes. But then Jesus will go further than Solomon can. Jesus will stand beneath the sun with us. From there he will look us in the eye and declare what Solomon cannot. "But take heart," Jesus will say; "I have overcome the world" (John 16:33).

QUESTIONS FOR DISCUSSION

1. Describe the kind of "gain" that Ecclesiastes sets in front of us.

2. How is it that the statement "Everything is meaningless" is actually quite meaningful?
3. What does it feel like to recognize that our lives fade
from memory?
4. In what ways are we limited as human creatures in
comparison to God?
5. What kind of hope are we meant to find in this chapter? How does this approach to hope differ from what
you are accustomed to?
6. How does the Preacher point us to the character of
God in Jesus?

CHAPTER FOUR

HANDLING OUR PLEASURES

"Whoever wishes to enjoy himself, falls."[1]

We sometimes talk to ourselves. Like Hannah, in the Old Testament, we speak in our heart; our lips move, but our voice is not heard (1 Sam. 1:13).

Likewise, in the New Testament, I do not know if anyone saw the suffering woman's lips move. But when she talked to herself, just before she crawled to touch the hem of Jesus' robe, she told herself of the hope she has in Jesus (Matt. 9:21).

Where I live, a haggard man with a rusty shopping cart reminds me of this woman. While it is not always easy or comfortable to sort out the code of his language, it seems that mostly he talks to himself about Jesus. There in the Walgreen's parking lot on Brentwood Boulevard, he preaches as if the pews are empty except for his own. But while we hold receipts in our hands and carry our shampoo or cough medicine to our cars, his soliloquy of divine promises reaches our ears.

Sometimes like this man, what we say to ourselves becomes audible. We don't realize that we are talking out loud or that someone else can hear us. Sometimes our thoughts are like the spy who lit a match in the dark and gave away his position.

In Ecclesiastes, the Preacher reminds us that he too has talked to himself (Eccl. 1:16; 2:15; 3:17–18). As "the greatest of all books of philosophy,"[2] Ecclesiastes is not academic and technical. It flows rather from a man who has long talked to himself in order to make sense of what he daily experiences under the sun. He is trying to sort out what those experiences tell him about the world, about God, and about himself. Unlike a political leader who, when out of office, writes a memoir in order to shore up his legacy, this king no longer trusts or needs our applause. It is as if he opens his diary and reads to us about how what he had said to himself let him down.

ENJOYING OURSELVES

> I said in my heart, "Come now, I will test you with pleasure; enjoy yourself." (Eccl. 2:1)

Solomon knew firsthand what it meant to be tested. The same Hebrew word used here in Ecclesiastes 2:1 is used to describe what happened to him in 1 Kings 10:1. "Now when the queen of Sheba heard of the fame of Solomon concerning the name of the Lord, she came to test him with hard questions."

Just as the queen of Sheba wanted to see what Solomon was truly like by traveling to where he was, spending time within his presence, and observing what her questions evoked from him, so Solomon now will test pleasures by going to them, spending time with them, and observing what becomes of him with them.

I live between the Mississippi and Missouri rivers, bodies of water once known only to God and to the Native Americans who canoed and fished them. Long ago, Lewis and Clark tested these waterways without knowing what awaited them around each bend and turn. I wonder, were they like my kids when they were toddlers in the world and scared to test in their mouths any food that smelled, looked, or felt foreign to them? Did they boldly taste a pea or lima bean or piece of kale the first time they laid eyes on them? Testing, after all, means experimenting in order to learn the nature of the thing.

In that vein, the Preacher determines to test the various kinds of joys being sold in the markets. He will put his paddle into their waters, their vegetables into his mouth. His goal however is not simply to learn his personal tastes, like one who takes a test online to determine what style of home decor she prefers. He states plainly that his purpose is to test his own heart. "I said in my heart, 'Come, now I will test you . . .'" The Preacher wants to learn how his heart will respond to those things under the sun that attempt to pleasure it. By doing so, the Bible raises a question in Ecclesiastes 2 that every human being asks, "Is there a thing in the world that can truly satisfy the heart of a human being?"

With this universal question in mind, we now begin to recognize that the Preacher in Ecclesiastes is not the prodigal son that Jesus teaches us about (Luke 15:11–32). Though they both will come to similar conclusions, their motives and purposes are distinct.

The prodigal gorges on pleasures because he believes that this is his right. He sells what belongs to him in order to get women or drink or friends for happiness. The Preacher, in contrast, seems to doubt whether this interior hole in his life can find anything to fill it. By wisdom he tests his theory and weathers the truth of it.

The prodigal consumes what is under the sun. The Preacher contends with it.

The prodigal loses his senses and must come to them again. The Preacher keeps his wits about him. He knows that both pleasure and poison reside among the mushrooms. So, for him, trying to pleasure one's heart? "This also" is "vanity" (Eccl. 2:1).

Few of us believe what the Preacher or the prodigal try to show us from their experiences. Fewer still address these questions of our enjoyment as purposefully as the Preacher. But most of us know full well what it is to talk to ourselves and to say, "Indulge yourself; pleasures are yours for the taking; enjoy yourself."

Foraging for pleasures we rebel as teenagers or in our midlife crisis. On our walls we put up posters or take them down, take our jobs and leave them, drink our booze or give it up. We take our medicine or quit it, we undress with strangers or refuse to do so, marry our spouses or leave them, have our kids or estrange them. We dye our hair or leave it natural, change our clothes or garage sale them, save our money or spend it; all of us hoping that in some gas station in life, a figurative or literal lottery ticket with a winning number waits for us to find it.

Finding it will elude us, however. Why? Because to "enjoy oneself" is to drink in what only the self can provide. Created beings and things only have so much that they can offer us. A video game may offer thirty-six unbelievable levels and absorb a young man's whole attention. But once the levels are overcome the man will pine for a new game, bored with what once thrilled him. Left to ourselves, our entertainment abilities are substantial but limited.

It isn't therefore that the Preacher disparages joy or the idea that we are meant to possess it. In fact, as we will see in a later chapter, joy is a gift from God that we are meant to receive. The problem has to do with where we look to enjoy ourselves along with the kinds of joy that we expect to find there.

"Whatever my eyes desired I did not keep from them," he tells us. "I kept my heart from no pleasure" (Eccl. 2:10). The Preacher now boils our possible joys down to the handful that actually exist. These levels in life are marvelous, good-feeling, and able to absorb us. But once we've played them, there is no other game. A woman stranded on an island may possess three board games, Yahtzee, Scrabble, and Sorry. Every night, there are always options for fun! But the options never change on an island she cannot leave. To enjoy oneself under the sun is like this. Gain eludes us in our pleasures.

FUN AND GAMES

So, in Ecclesiastes 2, the Preacher basically tells us that life under the sun always has nine basic amusements available for us on its closet shelves. Therefore, our options for a high under the sun always abound! But take note. The same old closet has offered these same nine games to every generation under the sun. These games are fun, but they are very old, tattered, and badly worn with use. Oh, and these are the only games in town.

- Jokes (Eccl. 2:2)
- Alcohol (Eccl. 2:3) *Food + Drink*
- Art (Eccl. 2:4)
- Nature (Eccl. 2:5–6)
- Money and possessions (Eccl. 2:7–8)
- Music (Eccl. 2:8)
- Sex (Eccl. 2:8)
- Affirmation (Eccl. 2:9)
- Work (Eccl. 2:11)

Intellectual
Sexual
psychological
spiritual

Relationships — children, grandchildren

Under the sun, we scavenger hunt for happy things; ancient, this scrounging (Gen. 3:6).

Health + Fitness

HANDLING OUR LAUGHTER

I had the hiccups once. For a remedy, an old adage suggests either holding one's breath or having someone frighten you when you least expect it. My five-year-old wanted to help. Frantically, with furrowed little brows and

65

bits of this old adage nestled in his young memory, he took my hand and urgently gave me this advice. "Dad, just hold your breath and scare somebody!" Then he said it again with emphasis. "Hold your breath and scare somebody!"

We all laughed so hard that we cried. Then after we all quieted into a pause, I hiccupped again.

Laughter is a wonderful gift. The Preacher teaches us that there are times under the sun in which the only appropriate way to respond is to laugh (Eccl. 3:4). Laughter gives expression to the language of joy. Wordless, it utters the glad sounds of mirth with God, our world, and each other (Ps. 126:1–3; Prov. 8:29–31).

Folk wisdom suggests that laughter is a good medicine. Abraham Lincoln, whose temperament made depression a long part of his daily life echoed the sentiment.

> If it were not for these stories—jokes—jests I should
>   die.
> They give vent—are the vents for my moods and
>   gloom.[3]

But even though laughter is good and possesses medicinal properties, it cannot fully heal us from what ails us under the sun. "Even in laughter the heart may ache" (Prov. 14:13). Therefore the Preacher tells us, "I said of laughter, 'it is mad' " (Eccl. 2:2).

Some forms of laughter expose its madness. In his monastic rule, Benedict notes plainly, "We condemn jokes and idle gossip and anything said to make others laugh."[4] What Benedict exaggerates nonetheless informs. At our worst, we are prone to squeeze the juices out of laughter's rind in order to attempt escape, excuse our sin, or promote folly. These kinds of laughter are not the sanest of friends.

For example, the escapist is always laughing, joking, and giggling; trying to urge others to smile even when the time for laughter has clocked out and the time to mourn has arrived. Laughter, in this case, chooses opposite to what the heart truly needs.

> Whoever sings songs to a heavy heart
>> is like one who takes off a garment on a cold day,
>> and like vinegar on soda. (Prov. 25:20)

Or, when old friends reunite for a weekend, the sharing of memories old and fond can belly laugh them. But sooner or later, the telling of old stories year upon year will not permit the friendships to grow deeper. New stories must get their turn at driving. Old laughters must hand over the keys. Likewise, relationships built around quoting comic lines from shared movies must sooner or later come out of the cinema into the unscripted day of doing a life together that isn't virtual. Laughter has its place on the stage of our lives, but it must learn to yield the spotlight to other necessary roles. We who laugh must learn also to let a season of weeping go uncomfortably unjoked.

Laughter can also become a tool for folly. We make jokes about things that ought to shame us. We puke drunk and giggle about it. This kind of laughter is like sharp thorns that bust holes, break the pot, and leave the soil to fall out and the plant roots abandoned. Trying to mend this plant bleeds the fingers (Eccl. 7:6).

Laughter can also excuse our mistreatment of a family member or neighbor. Instead of saying that we are sorry and need to grow, we blame-shift and say, "Lighten up!"

> Like a madman who throws firebrands, arrows, and
> death is the man who deceives his neighbor and
> says, "I am only joking!" (Prov. 26:18–19)

Laughter can bless us. Many of us need more of its medicine. But while we dwell under the sun, "sorrow is better than laughter" (Eccl. 7:3). Jesus, full of joy, was

67

nonetheless the "man of sorrows" (Isa. 53:3). There will come a time in which all tears will be wiped away and the glad laughter of true joy will rest within our hearts unimpeded. But too much ache remains under the sun just yet. Laughter cannot save. It too needs a Savior.

ALCOHOL AND SEX

In 1633, pastor George Herbert wrote an extensive poem in order to aid his congregation in the grace of Jesus. Part of his poetry addressed both the goodness and the trap of alcohol.

> Drink not the third glass, which thou canst not tame,
>   once it is
> within thee . . . Shall I to please another's wine-
>   sprung mind
> lose all my own . . .?[5]

The king contends with drink, keeps his sobriety, and tests it out to see what joy his heart can find in it. "I searched with my heart how to cheer my body with wine—my heart still guiding me with wisdom"(Eccl. 2:3). Like Herbert's poem, the pastor takes up his glass but knows when to put it down, his "heart still guiding" him wisely. Even if the Preacher had been drunk, his point would remain.

Wine can give us a "merry heart" (Eccl. 9:7). Wine "gladdens life" (Eccl. 10:19). But wine is a poor lover, "a mocker," "a brawler," that leads us astray (Prov. 20:1).

> Who has woe? Who has sorrow?
>   Who has strife? Who has complaining?
> Who has wounds without cause?
>   Who has redness of eyes?
> Those who tarry long over wine. (Prov. 23:29–30)

What if beer commercials during sports events portrayed this? Imagine a halftime commercial at the Super Bowl that showed an Alcoholics Anonymous meeting, or a wasted man hugging a toilet at 3:00 A.M., or a woman who got drunk for a stranger but then was abandoned after use in a hotel, or a scene with a drunken father raging and violent toward his wife and kids, or an alcoholic losing his job. Wine and beer are a gift. But buzzing for happiness leaves us thirsty. And, according to the Preacher, even a modest enjoyment of wine with our wits intact can delight us, but not with the gain we long for.

In Nehemiah, the people of God are urged to "eat the fat and drink sweet wine" as a way of celebrating the holiness of the day. However, this comes with the reminder that true strength is found in "the joy of the LORD" (Neh. 8:10).

The prophet Isaiah calls out to us therefore.

> Come, everyone who thirsts,
> come to the waters;
> and he who has no money,
> come, buy and eat!
> Come, buy wine and milk
> without money and without price.
> Why do you spend your money for that which is
> not bread,
> and your labor for that which does not satisfy?
> Listen diligently to me, and eat what is good,
> and delight yourselves in rich food. (Isa. 55:1–2)

A kind of food and drink exists that comes from God and satisfies (see also Eph. 5:18). Jesus stands up in the midst of a great celebratory feast and says, "If anyone thirsts, let him come to me and drink" (John 7:37). The Preacher wants us to know that neither the connoisseur nor the drunkard can find true gain in the glass.

Sometimes the glass and sex combine. A woman might drink so that she can make sexual choices that she never would while sober. A certain kind of man knows this and offers her another drink. Both the man and the woman understand that this kind of physical sex needs the help of some booze. Drink replaces love, impaired thinking replaces covenant. A one-night stand awaits. The bed empties in the morning. Two strangers go their separate ways. In her book *Loose Girl: A Memoir of Promiscuity*, Kerry Cohen chronicles the emptiness that a life of sex with multiple men eventually brought her. She not only literally loses track of their names, but she begins to lose track of hers too—who she is and what she was meant for. "For a man this might be a pleasant trip down memory lane, counting up his conquests," she writes. "But for a girl, it's a whole other story. I had let these men inside me, wanting that to make me matter to them. Wanting it to make me matter."[6]

Solomon tells us that as king, he had "many concubines" (Eccl. 2:8). He could locker-room boast and win. He knew the company of many different women and could indulge himself if he desired. Solomon lived the fantasy of many men and women. He makes a woman feel that she is one of the chosen among women, different to him than the other women he could have who are in his kingdom. He makes a man feel it is possible to have lots of women ready and willing to satisfy his sexual desires.

But apart from this, even the covenant goodness of sexual intimacy as described in the Song of Solomon isn't the provider of our ultimate gain. Let's say that last night, husband and wife made love the way God intended for them—full of passion, delight, and the pornless enjoyment of one another's nakedness. The young married couple slept peacefully in each other's arms. This morning the alarm clock still sounds; the diapers, traffic, and bills are waiting.

Deep into middle age and fully one with the wide smile of their satisfying bodily love, they reach for their robes and the bones pop, the joints ache. Even the wonder of sex the way it was meant to be cannot bring about the gain we lack under the sun. Under the sun something more is necessary for true gain.

ART, CREATIVITY, MUSIC, AND NATURE

The Preacher now turns his attention to the things he made. "I made great works," he says (Eccl. 2:4). The Preacher's grounds became his gallery. One could walk through his yards and marvel at his creations. As an artist, an architect, and a designer, he created a plan for how he wanted things to look and to work. He imagined it, thrust his hands into the clay, and sculpted what he conceptualized into being.

As we already discussed in our previous chapter, some are tempted to look in vain to one's yard for gain. Nature itself offers pleasure to us and Solomon tested it out. "I made myself gardens and parks," he says, "and planted in them all kinds of fruit trees. I made myself pools from which to water the forest of growing trees" (Eccl. 2:5–6). But we also add our own works to the creation around us.

At Christmastime twenty minutes' drive from my house, the front yard of a local man draws people from all over the St. Louis area. Model train tracks blanket and crisscross the yard, along with his meticulous re-creations of houses, people, parks, and churches. The multiple trains run their routes through basement windows and back again through tunnels as we on the sidewalks drink hot chocolate and marvel at the work the man has made. What a joy it is to take our kids, and what a pleasure it must be for this man to create what he loves and to see others blessed by it.

Not far from this man's front yard and his trains, the St. Louis Gateway Arch towers high into the skyline to be viewed by all who cross the Mississippi River to enter or leave this Gateway city to the West. Not far from the Arch stands the City Museum, an enormous playland for kids made from city trash and leftovers such as old chimneys, bridges, abandoned planes, tiles, stairs, and buses. It astonishes us.

In our hands, our works join nature for our pleasure. Metals, cloth, wood, paint, film, paper, or even bottle caps become materials that we use to create. The Preacher enjoyed such creativity, and all who came to visit his place would have noticed. And yet, "there was nothing to be gained under the sun" (Eccl. 2:11).

The Preacher agrees with lovers of art, design, architecture, and creativity in their delight. But the Preacher finds no lasting gain in it. For him, art offers meaning and beauty. Like laughter, it offers medicinal value and companions us well.

But the Preacher challenges the idea that sometimes tempts us to look for salvation in our great works. This idea can sound like this: "After one has abandoned a belief in god, poetry is that essence which takes its place as life's redemption."[7]

Human hands can create words on a page, airplanes, and marvelous towers. But our creativity cannot stop airplanes from flying into two such towers in order to live out someone's poetry. Artwork hung on the walls that day while the rubble crashed into the city on September 11. Similarly, in time, a foreign power would occupy, own, and trash Solomon's great works. Today, most of them are gone.

We, and what we create, resemble the marvelous but troubled Dutch artist, Vincent van Gogh. He painted majestic beauty from within an asylum. The paintings bless and reveal, but they cannot preserve our sanity. We must wait for gain from another source.

Music and songwriters also give us pleasure and point us to meaningful joys. Solomon knew this. "I got singers, both men and women" (Eccl. 2:8). Solomon put in a living sound system and piped the music throughout his landscape. As people walked to enjoy the gallery, they could enjoy the beauty of human voice, the stirrings of melody, the foot taps of rhythm. Music evokes memory and stirs imagination. It has universal appeal and gives common language to those whose cultures and languages differ. I've seen its medicinal value holding the hand of the dying in hospice.

I also know what it is to look to music to make my heart whole. As a young man, I would turn up the radio, close my eyes, and lose myself in voice, melody, and rhythm.

When the song ends, we have to open our eyes again. The sunless morning still waits for us to enter it. The dishes dirty in the sink still wait for soap.

MONEY, POSSESSIONS, FAME, AND OUR WORK

"Why Are Americans So Unhappy?"[8] This headline is not unique, as many doctors, sociologists, and others try to grapple with the strange irony that many Americans feel. We are among the wealthiest and most privileged peoples in the world, but we are far less content and rarely as happy as those who possess a fraction of what we do.

Since the time when Adam and Eve believed that they needed one more tree than they had and that their lives were incomplete unless they could have one more kind of fruit, the human soul has been prone to take the pleasure that money can provide as a sign that money itself constitutes true gain in life. Many of us build our whole lives around a pursuit of getting more for tomorrow than we have today. The Preacher tells us about this same pursuit of money and possessions in his own life.

> I bought male and female slaves, and had slaves who were born in my house. I had also great possessions of herds and flocks, more than any who had been before me in Jerusalem. I also gathered for myself silver and gold and the treasure of kings and provinces. (Eccl. 2:7–8)

The Preacher captures what the heart wants. He had power over other people. Though the kind of slavery mentioned here differs in kind from slavery in America's history, the principle remains inhumanely the same; one person is owned by another like property. Throughout history human beings show a desire to own others, to boss them, and to have the power to dictate to others the service we want for ourselves. We rightly react and want to "stick it to the man."

By analogy, those who have employees want more and can treat employees as if their livelihood and personal life depends upon their doing solely what the owner dictates. Possessions and money join this kind of power and form the dream to which every generation of nations, groups, families, and individuals aspires for gain. Wars, crimes, theft, murders, family feuds, betrayals of friendship, parents growing up without knowing their kids, kids growing up neglected or bribed and entitled; these flow from greed, covetousness, discontentment, envy, and the dream of wealth and power.

Solomon had it all, and he concludes that money, power, and possessions cannot satisfy us or rescue the world.

> He who loves money will not be satisfied with money, nor he who loves wealth with his income. . . . When goods increase, they increase who eat them, and what advantage has their owner but to see them with his eyes? (Eccl. 5:10–11)

To see our work with our eyes is the reward or gain we get. A man works all of his life with a company. He retires, receives a pen and a pat on the back. That moment of seeing the work is the best the work can offer. She makes jewelry and scarves, and markets them. She gets to see someone wear what she made. That moment of seeing is a wonderful gift but the only advantage that her labor can offer her. For this reason, affirmation and fame feel wonderful, but each is a gypsy—a wanderer who fidgets to leave as soon as it arrives. "So I became great and surpassed all who were before me in Jerusalem," the Preacher says (Eccl. 2:9). But this too was its own reward.

DEATH

I once quarterbacked a state championship football team. It was awesome! That was thirty years ago. I was in junior high.

Last night, we had a few dollars in our pockets. It felt good to buy a Frosty at Wendy's for our kids and us. This morning we woke up hungry—the Frosties and the dollars already spent.

I greatly enjoy the house that I rent. I hope that I can buy it someday. But even if I do, there is a mouse in the walls, and the house won't parent my kids in my absence or show me the way to God.

When my mamaw and papaw died, I received an old leather chair, a pocketknife, and a raincoat. I treasure these, but I wonder if these were treasures to them? Even if they were, Mamaw and Papaw are gone from this world. Someday I too will be gone, and what will become of their leather chair and the raincoat?

The Preacher raises this point. Death is the trump card upon all of these pleasures under the sun. It is not that they aren't enjoyable; they are. But laughter, alcohol, art, nature, money, possessions, power, cannot stop death from coming. Even if we are wise and we avoid using the good things of this world as substitute saviors, even our being wise about it all cannot bring us the gain we need.

So I turned about and gave my heart up to despair over all the toil of my labors under the sun, because sometimes a person who has toiled with wisdom and knowledge and skill must leave everything

75

to be enjoyed by someone who did not toil for it. (Eccl. 2:20–21)

When we were young, we dreamt of a house to buy, a yard to create with, pieces of furniture to possess, and a bank account from which to use for our gain. When we are old, a time comes to sell everything that once represented our dreams of a future. We have to move to an assisted living facility, or in with our kids while someone else uses the drapes we left on the windows we used to wash and enjoy.

A young woman fills a hope chest with treasures over which she dreams, and intends to bring into her future with her man. An elderly woman has long since buried her lovely man and now has to sell or give her hope chest away.

As he came from his mother's womb he shall go again, naked as he came, and shall take nothing for his toil that he may carry away in his hand. (Eccl. 5:15)

The One greater than Solomon takes up this truth and preaches it. There are treasures, so called, that last for a moment but rust and moth eat away. Other treasures exist of a kind that rust and moth cannot touch. The former make us smile, but they cannot keep the frowns of the world from taking place. A treasure of a different kind is needed that can outlast this life under the sun (Matt. 6:19–20).

The house my papaw built with his own hands now sits among the pine trees, shelving another man's toolbox.

CONCLUSION

In his essay, "The Weight of Glory," C. S. Lewis famously addressed our gainless search among the joys offered to us under the sun.

We are half-hearted creatures, fooling about with drink and sex and ambition when infinite joy is offered us, like an ignorant child who wants to go on making mud pies in a slum because he cannot imagine what is meant by the offer of a holiday at the sea. We are far too easily pleased.[9]

Lewis echoes part of the Preacher's haunting implication. Even though there are these pleasures in the world that are ours for use, they cannot satisfy what only God can.

First, even wisdom along with the proper use of created joys cannot spare us from what happens under the sun. The wise will die just like the fool. Even if one wisely turns from mud pies to God, life under the sun will not necessarily reward them for it. Neither the foolish use of sex nor the proper enjoyment of it can save us. Because one chooses not to drink, or to drink wisely, will not prove to be the answer that the situation under the sun ultimately needs for it to change. Hedonism won't work. But neither will morality, no matter how much better morality is. We will have to look beyond both for true gain. Neither the wisdom nor the folly of human beings can make the world right again. Only a righteousness from heaven will do this.

Second, the Preacher wants us to feel sad about this. He wants us to see how far from Eden we have come. Once it was enough for a man and a woman to have God and the good gifts that God gave, even if it meant that there was a tree and a fruit that existed but not for them. Now, even though we are surrounded by opportunities to laugh, or drink, or work, or make money, none of it is enough, we are not satisfied, and death stomps on all of it. Even our marvelous moments of good work and good intimacy with the lover of our lives will one day become only a memory and then gone forever in the world.

Death did this to us. We did this to us. God let it be. He will have to take care of death and all that has flown from it. In time he will. In time the promised One will come. A cross will stand. A tomb will empty and death will die.

QUESTIONS FOR DISCUSSION

1. How does the Preacher of Ecclesiastes resemble and differ from the prodigal son in Jesus' story?
2. Choose one of the pleasures listed—jokes (Eccl. 2:2), alcohol (Eccl. 2:3), art (Eccl. 2:4), nature (Eccl. 2:5–6), money and possessions (Eccl. 2:7–8), music (Eccl. 2:8), sex (Eccl. 2:8), affirmation (Eccl. 2:9), work (Eccl. 2:11)—and talk about the role it has played in your life. How does Ecclesiastes both affirm and warn you about this "pleasure"?
3. How does death make earthly joys ultimately unsatisfying?
4. How do we relate to Jesus in light of these earthly pleasures and in light of death?

CHAPTER FIVE

HATING LIFE AND
BEING WISE

"Every lament is a love song."[1]

Imagine a grandson home from college and visiting for the holiday. The visit has been lovely but way too short. Standing on the porch, the grandmother and the grandson share a look together in a quiet pause. Before he gets into his car for the drive west, all eyes, both young and old, water. The tears that snatch the words rise from two sources. One, the irritation that life as it is requires such sad good-byes. Two, the grateful gift it was to enjoy a couple of ordinary days together.

It is strange to witness sad hatred and grateful love in conversation. Their voices contradict and interrupt each other. Yet, both responses tangle, for example, when Jesus visits the tomb of his friend Lazarus. Jesus sees everyone aching and weeping in light of Lazarus having died. He is "deeply moved in his spirit and greatly troubled" (John 11:33). The Greek word used to describe this deep inward movement indicates strong irritation, scolding, and near anger. The scene of death and separated friendship rouses Jesus' indignation. He hates the presence of it all. Meanwhile, shortly thereafter, the shortest verse in the Bible reveals the presence of his love for Lazarus and the life they knew together. "Jesus wept," it says. And those watching said, "See how he loved him!" (John 11:35–36).

We can imagine that both of those opposite sentiments merged again in the grandson as he too stood at the graveside when his grandmother died. He hates death. He despairs at the separation. He is deeply irritated and angry at it all. At the same time, he remembers shared moments of love. He weeps and weeps with gratitude and longing.

In Ecclesiastes 2 so far, the Preacher has taken an inventory of gainless joys. He has strewn them one by one across his yard, while the grave is on his mind. Now what? How does wisdom respond to the meaninglessness of pleasures? As he stands on his porch surveying the tattered scene, it looks to the Preacher like a circus floor littered with empty peanut shells. Viewing this scene results in his desire to give us some advice. When you see the world in light of the grave, two responses are required. The first is hatred. The second is enjoyment. If we are to grow wise in response to life as it is under the sun, we need the spiritual skill of both.

In this chapter, we will focus first on this wisdom way of hating. In the following chapter, we will think through what the Preacher then says about grateful enjoyment.

THE STRONG MAN CRIES

When his grandpa wept at the graveside, the grandson was disoriented. He'd never seen the strong man cry. Likewise, when the Preacher says, "I hated life," it disorients us. We do not expect to hear a Bible preacher publicly announce his distaste for his life and work. Our expectations for those who follow and speak for God more often resemble the picture offered by an employee at a local Christian bookstore near my first pastorate. When asked how one was doing, she always beamed and vibrantly announced, "I'm blessed!" Or at a local restaurant associated with Christians every employee will smile and tell you repeatedly that it is their pleasure always to serve.

If all of our days are only blessings and pleasures, then it will tempt some of us to dismiss Solomon, to rebuke him, to quote to him or exhort him to greater faith. Prone to believe that his talk about hating life reveals immaturity at its worst or burnout and depression at its best, we might want to ask the Preacher to step down from this pulpit. We might want to turn off his sermons and turn instead to more comforting messages in other books of the Bible. After all, while we seek a healthier, more mature teacher to replace him, he can get the help he needs, and we can get back to learning about the happy faith and dynamic hope that God's people are meant to have.

Yet Solomon's language resembles the rest of the Bible's wisdom literature. We learn from such books and such language that the life of faith includes these untidy sentiments. For example, in the book of Job, the Psalms, Proverbs, and Ecclesiastes, God gives us categories for faith that include the capacity for all ranges of emotion and thought. Faithful despair, wise hatred, hallowed hollering, and good complaint rise for our mentoring.

Job opens his mouth for all to hear. He curses the day of his birth. "Let the day perish on which I was born," he says. "Let that day be darkness! Let God above not seek it, nor light shine upon it" (Job 3:4). And Job testifies that nothing helps him. "If I speak, my pain is not assuaged, and if I forbear, how much of it leaves me?" Far from testifying to being blessed, Job declares, "Surely now God has worn me out; he has made desolate all my company" (Job 16:6–7).

The psalmists also vent their desperate fatigue with no relief under the sun.

> Reproaches have broken my heart,
>   so that I am in despair.

> I looked for pity, but there was none,
>> and for comforters, but I found none. (Ps. 69:20)

> My soul refuses to be comforted.
> When I remember God, I moan;
>> when I meditate, my spirit faints. Selah.
>>> (Ps. 77:2–3)

And yet we are told that Job is a righteous man of faith, defended in all he has said by God himself (Job 1:1; 42:7–8). Likewise, it is King David and Asaph who wrote these psalms. Their words are God breathed.

When men of faith such as Job and King David speak in such ugly ways, they foreshadow moments infinitely more strange to our ears. Jesus, our Redeemer, sweats like blood and in despair asks God if possible to find a way forward that does not require the slanders, the betrayals, the beatings, and the cross (Mark 14:36). Then, while weaker men of faith taunt him to reveal the strength of his own, Jesus exposes a profound complaint to God for all, including his enemies, to hear. "My God, my God, why have you forsaken me?" (Matt. 27:46).

What is Jesus doing on a cross speaking with such doubt and pain in the presence of those demanding an answer and a sign? Shouldn't he have had more faith and preached the good news of blessing and hope to all who listened? What kind of uninviting message are we sending about life with God if we enter such violent places and there use such gloomy speech? An old bit of poetry comes to mind.

> All that is gold does not glitter,
> Not all those who wander are lost.[2]

This Preacher in Ecclesiastes is in good company, the company of the wise and faithful. "I hated life," he says, and the gold of the wise lies buried within these blackened walls of char and ash.

GOD

To begin, the Preacher hates life, not God. Solomon announces his hatred for life from a God-centered podium. Like other biblical sages, he orients his life and teaching from the vantage point of the fear of the Lord (Eccl. 12:13). This means that the existence, character, and communication of God form the reference point for the Preacher's thoughts and words.

We know this because Solomon seeks to furnish our minds with the contemplation of God. Over thirty times in these twelve chapters, the Preacher exalts God as our Creator, gift giver, enjoyment provider, life sustainer, wisdom teacher, Redeemer, and judge. The Preacher intends that upon hearing his message, his audience will contemplate God. Even the Preacher's statements of hating life remind us, then, of what John Calvin once earlier introduced to us.

> We are prompted by our own ills to contemplate the
>   good things of God;
> and we cannot seriously aspire to him before we
>   begin to become displeased with ourselves.[3]

What does this teach us? Distressing words needn't signify the absence of faith. Sometimes, in fact, it is faith itself that encourages our voices to utter our sores and our aches.

> In my distress I called upon the Lord;
>   to my God I cried for help.
> From his temple he heard my voice,
>   and my cry to him reached his ears. (Ps. 18:6)

We cast our cares, "because he cares for" us (1 Peter 5:7). In our groanings too deep for words, he too groans and helps us in our weakness (Rom. 8:26).

Likewise, speaking what troubles us needn't indicate our immaturity. Sometimes only the mature have the capacity to resist denial or pretense and to admit things as they truly are. It is in our time of need that we come before his throne of grace for help (Heb. 4:16).

If a child believes that her parents cannot handle what she actually questions or feels, she will pretend all is well or constantly tantrum about. But she will not reveal her true heart in all of its nobility and ugliness; needy for help, longing to try, rotting with secrets. But show her a parent who has a capacity for her, and she will risk, argue, ask, laugh, learn, and cry in the presence of their love.

God holds us together, even the vexed and harassed among us. The wise who believe this learn not to fear revealing what is true about their despair or hatred. God's character and covenant anchor their voice and make every feeling and thought, no matter how beautiful or foul, a matter of prayer for God to enter, of presence with God to keep, of paraphernalia for God to redeem.

The abused don't talk back, except finally to rage when the last straw breaks. But the rage isn't faith. The rage is all smokescreen and walls, barbed wire and electric fence to keep the wolves out. The Preacher doesn't have to rage. He simply speaks plainly to us and to God without denial, manipulation, exaggeration, minimization, self-protection, or pretense. "I hated life," he admits. God could handle him saying this.

Similarly, the constantly accused do not reveal their worst moments. Worst moments are all that the suspicious remember. But Solomon has a whole life of prayers, victories, agonies, and sins before God. To say that he hates life doesn't mean that he always did or always will. The Preacher's life doesn't rise or fall on this one sentence and this one season but on God's character and history toward both Solomon and the world. So it is with how God relates to us.

All this is to say that the wise learn to manage life, not by frantically trying to glue together the knocked-over vase, but by gathering all of the shattered jagged pieces and powdered dust from the floor and bringing them then to God.

Consequently, Solomon speaks like this, not just because God can handle it but because a true relationship with God sometimes requires such language. Otherwise, we compartmentalize the ugly within us and act as if the world is not broken. We only tell God that we are blessed and full of pleasure to serve. We take our pains and frustrations and hide them away when all along we could have brought them to God and encouraged others to do the same. The Preacher mentors us into a life that places God at the center of everything, even of our hatreds. A God-fearing Preacher, in his maturity, can say, "I hated life."

WISELY HATING

We learn then how the wise are meant to hate. What does this mean?

The same shirt on a man of bulk will drape the body differently when worn by a stick man. Likewise, King Saul's armor highlighted his handsome regality. But the same armor when placed on David only avalanched his body with metal and left him longing for a bare arm and a small stone from the river brook. The same cloth changes shape according to the proportions of the one who wears it. So it is with hatred and the one who puts it on.

But hatred carries itself differently on a man of wisdom, not only because the wise wear it contrarily from how others do, but also because the hatred of the wise differs in kind from the rancor of the fool. Folly sees all kinds of hatreds on sale and buys them. But wisdom will pass by a bargain when the thing bargained for is no good from the start. Hatred comes then in many forms. But wisdom has eyes for only one of them. The Preacher in Ecclesiastes introduces us to that one hatred which the wise willingly take up.

So, I hated life, *because what is done under the sun was grievous to me, for all is vanity and a striving after wind.* I hated all my toil in which I toil under the sun, seeing that I must leave it to the man who will come after me, and who knows whether he will be wise or a fool? (Eccl. 2:17–19)

The word *grievous* has the idea of bad, severe, or evil. The Preacher says that that which is done under the sun is distasteful and worthy of tears. The fact that the wise die just like the foolish. The reality that everything is worn out and groaning in creation along with our aching human search for empty gain in drink, nature, laughter, sex, work, affirmation, music, money, and the like. The harm that people do to one another; the plight and condition of human beings; the frustrating business that God has not removed from us; the eventual loss of everything worked for and the prospect that no one will remember us; this condition of things signifies what the Preacher hates.

The Preacher therefore does not describe depression here. Some hate life and want to die.

Elijah wanted to die because exhaustion, trauma, and fear told him that he was despised and alone. Self-pity awoke like a dragon in the cave of his being. What Elijah needed was rest, food, and a strong taming of this fire-breathing sense that he alone was left to care about God in the world (1 Kings 19:4ff.). Jonah wanted to die because he hated the people God called him to love and the sermons God called him to preach. Anger ate him up on the inside. He would rather drown than change. He needed time, the words of God, and grace upon grace upon grace (Jonah 4:3). Job too makes known his wish that God would just let him die (Job 6:8–10). The painful loss of his family and his livelihood and the constant suffering from his own bodily disease lead him to ask God to crush him.

But Solomon isn't grieving due to spiritual hardness, self-pity, terrible loss, or psychotic, emotional, or circumstantial depression. When he says, "I hated life," he differs from these others in this. The Westminster Larger Catechism describes the miserable realities of Eden lost. In this world under the sun, there exists, "blindness of mind, a reprobate sense, strong delusions, hardness of heart, horror of conscience, and vile affections," along with "other evils that befall us in our bodies, names, estates, relations, and employments; together with death itself."[4] The Preacher tells us plainly that he hates this state of things. This state of things grieves him. He watches the news and weeps. He himself sins against others and longs for an end to this way of doing life.

We read the news. We bury our children. Murders, thefts, bribes, fists, weapons, sex, lies, and weather patterns are used to brutalize people. We watch the raping world. We hate that what God created good has become like a rusty-nailed playground no longer fit for kids at play and cutting the skin of those who try. We hate this. The wise cannot pretend that all is well.

So, when Solomon teaches us "that there is a time to hate" (Eccl. 3:8), he means that it is right and good to cultivate a distaste for the misery, the sin, the death, the evil and the havoc with which each of these ravages us. The Preacher could join the psalmist in song. "O you who love the LORD, hate evil!" (Ps. 97:10).

We hate death and the violence that neighbors inflict on others and against God. But before we spray-paint hate speech on our posters in God's name, we also understand why our neighbors also tire of us, with our own ability to inflict them with what is contrary to love, life, grace, and truth. The world groans, not only because of others, but also because of us. Eden wasn't like this. We hate that it has come to this.

In contrast to the Preacher, the fool teaches us to hate individual people, God, wisdom, love, wise correction, truth, beauty, and knowledge (Prov. 1:22; 9:8; 29:10; Tit. 3:3). Folly says to embrace bitter jealousy, selfish ambition, and partiality (James 3:14–16). It teaches us to cherish what Adam and Eve did and to hold onto the "desires of the flesh and the desires of the eyes and pride of life" (1 John 2:15–16). The preacher counters such folly with a call to wisdom. But what can wisdom do for us?

WHY BE WISE?

A poor man was very wise. He lived in a city of little consequence in the world. A mighty king came against these city inhabitants, and they were few in number. The royal man used his might and wealth to put the little city under siege. The poor man responded by his wisdom to the attack. In time, the poor man delivered the tiny city from the clutches of the bombastic king. Once free, none of the rescued city members remembered the poor man. They picked the apples of his wisdom but forgot how the root, the bark, the leafy branch, and the replenishing rain arrived there to begin with. So, the wise man with his wisdom nonetheless spent the rest of his days overlooked and underestimated in his community, not only because of his low position as a poor person among the well-to-do, but also in terms of the honor that was his due. Day by day, they passed him by, not knowing or seeing how indebted to him they actually were.

After telling this story, the Preacher declares: "But I say that wisdom is better than might, though the poor man's wisdom is despised and his words are not heard" (Eccl. 9:14–16).

Here in Ecclesiastes 2, and in Ecclesiastes 8–9, the Preacher therefore entertains the question, "Why be wise when it too, along with pleasures, will gain us nothing in the world?" We need not be afraid to ask hard questions. Wisdom shows us how.

Then I said in my heart, "What happens to the fool will happen to me also. *Why then have I been so very wise?"* And I said in my heart that this also is vanity. (Eccl. 2:15)

If no lasting gain exists under the sun, and nothing under the sun can change these conditions, and the wise ends up the same as the fool, then what is the point of being wise or good at all? The Preacher entertains the thought.

He admits that often under the sun, folly receives no tangible consequences.

> Then I saw the wicked buried. They used to go in and out of the holy place and were praised in the city where they had done such things. This also is vanity. Because the sentence against an evil deed is not executed speedily, the heart of the children of man is fully set to do evil. (Eccl. 8:10–11)

All of their lives these foolish ones went to church (the holy place). All of their lives these who cared nothing for wisdom were honored with public praise and reputation (praised in the city). Yet in truth they were wicked toward God and others. They were never caught; their folly received honor, their crimes remained unsolved, their victims remained mocked.

The Preacher notes that even when a person is caught in his wrongdoing, often the system slowly lumbers along. Years go by. The victim has to relive and retell the story over and again. Meanwhile, the perpetrator watches movies, enjoys food, has conjugal visits, and completes an educational degree. The Preacher admits what I myself have known. I stole a candy bar once. I was thirteen. I was never caught. The chocolate tasted good. Many people discover that when they finally do the thing they are not supposed to, no lightning strikes, no harm befalls, and they can still have their latte at Starbucks.

The rain falls upon the just
And also on the unjust fellas

But mostly it falls upon the just
Cause the unjust have the just's umbrellas.[5]

Another reason that we may want to forgo a life of wisdom has to do with the fact that being wise gives us no immunity under the sun. "The same event happens to the righteous and the wicked," he observes. "As the good one is, so is the sinner . . . the same event happens to all" (Eccl. 9:2–3). Even more, sometimes "there are righteous people to whom it happens according to the deeds of the wicked, and there are wicked people to whom it happens according to the deeds of the righteous" (Eccl. 8:14). Sometimes good people are treated poorly while the fool receives awards and honor.

Trying to pursue the virtue of wisdom doesn't mean that cancer, dementia, a flood, or a broken heart won't come to us. Tornados don't choose to hit only the "bad" houses in a region. My grandparents who love the Lord found themselves in a flooded region in Nashville, Tennessee. Many "Christians" descended upon those without electricity, or water or houses. Instead of raising their hands to help the downcast, they raised their posters and proclaimed God's judgment upon those people. According to them, Nashville got what it deserved because of its godless ways.

The Preacher in Ecclesiastes doesn't seem to see the hardship that people suffer under the sun that simply. The wise cannot bribe God for immunity under the sun. Even the very wise can scrape their knees or need a dentist or be sentenced to death unjustly upon a cross.

Wisdom therefore, though it is better than pleasure or might, is no savior. Therefore, those who try to be good and wise in order to get God to do favors for them or their kids or their friends under the sun will find disappointment.

Again I saw that under the sun the race is not to the swift, nor the battle to the strong, nor bread to the wise, nor riches to the intelligent, nor favor to those with knowledge, but time and chance happen to them all. (Eccl. 9:11)

Through the Preacher, God is teaching Israel that it lives in the same world as everybody else. God is not theirs so that they can have vacation days while the rest endure the afternoon. God cannot be used to get us gain in once-Eden. Remember, even the very wise will be forgotten here, and God will not stop that amnesia from happening (Eccl. 9:14–15).

So, it would seem that we should say, "If you can't beat it, join it!" Being wise will not guarantee justice, immunity, or advancement for you in the world, and folly is more fun anyway!

Yet, even though the Preacher admits the inability of wisdom to save or secure us, he nonetheless chooses wisdom as his way of life. By doing so, he answers our question: Why be good if it brings us no advantage, provides us no security, and cannot change the fallen conditions in this world? Why live as a wise man or woman if it will not alleviate our poverty, enable people to listen to us, or bring us the honor we are due by those whom we have served? Why not be rich, foolish, loud, honored, and listened to instead?

- Because wisdom by its nature is good and it alone brings us closer to the gain that we need (Eccl. 2:13–14). Therefore we resist folly because it is right to do so, whether it brings us honor in this life or not. We seek it for its own sake, not for what it will do for us.
- Because wisdom, though it may not change the world, does change us (Eccl. 8:1, 5). The damage of our hardened hearts, our misuse of neighbors, our flawed thinking, our empty search for gain, these all lessen with wisdom. We change and those who know us feel the difference. The city

is delivered because of how wisdom shaped an obscure man whom they forgot. The king of might is confounded. Rescue from such a king blesses even though such kings still exist in the world and cities still fall under siege.

- Because our lives are in God's hands and wisdom testifies to God's character under the sun (Eccl. 9:1). Though God does not stop the madness for now, he remains invested in it and with us under the sun. We seek wisdom because we seek to glorify him and to acknowledge that he sustains us.

- Because a wisdom way of life is better for people (Eccl. 9:16–18). When people are not misled, used, oppressed, or shouted at they experience pleasantness and strength—reminders of what we were meant to know.

- Because God will judge us and God loves wisdom (Eccl. 8:12–13). Folly boasts and brags. It wins and triumphs . . . for now. But the victories of folly are not eternal. Both the foolish and the wise will stand before God to give an account. The poor man, the rescued inhabitants, and the mighty oppressive king will all kneel before God. Folly will not have the last word.

The One greater than Solomon would come. He too would dwell as a poor man in a city. The city was physically and spiritually besieged as human and devilish powers sought to kill, steal, and destroy. Most did not listen. Most despised him. Most forgot him. But by him the rescue came.

MOUNTING A WISDOM RESISTANCE

Imagine a basketball team made up of seven- and eight-year-olds. One team cheats, trips, trash talks, and pushes. Imagine that the referees are friends of the cheating team's coaches. It becomes obvious that the referees are biased in favor of this cheating team. Now imagine that you coach the opposing team. What do you tell your players?

You can tell them to quit. You can say, "I hate this game! There is no point in trying because no matter what you do you will not win and you can get hurt in the process. Let's get out of here."

Or you can tell them to return the same kind of behavior. You can say to your team, "I hate this game! Since this is all unfair and no one seems to care, you do the same to them; you too need to cheat, trip, trash talk, and push. If the only way to get ahead is to break the rules, so be it!"

This Preacher looks at both options. He fully understands what it means to hate how the game is being played. But when he looks at walking away, this leaves folly to win on the court. Folly then becomes the only game in town. Likewise, when he looks at joining in and fighting folly with folly, this too leaves only folly on the court. Folly still remains the only game in town.

The Preacher agrees on the one hand; "I hate this life," he admits. But the response this kind of hatred promotes differs substantially from the other two. "I will oppose the life I hate with wisdom," he seems to say. "Not because I will win in this world. I likely will not. But at least wisdom will remain on the court. At least folly will no longer offer the only game in town. At least those who watch the game will have an alternative set in front of them, and those who play and get hurt will have a way of healing still available to them."

In essence, the Preacher changes the purpose for playing the game. He calls us to question the motive by which we seek God and the world. For the Preacher, we do not play to win or to advance or to gain for ourselves. We play because of God and because of what such a relationship with God establishes. In our clubs, our workplaces, our families, our blended families, our churches, our governments, and our neighborhoods, wisdom is the way that God's people choose to make a stand—even if it means that they are overlooked, undervalued, impoverished, slandered, forgotten, or misused. His notions are strange to us. He is saying that it is better to experience poverty, dismissal, and a life of forgotten service, than to find health, wealth, and happiness through foolish means and for a foolish purpose. Better to have Jesus and no money or status in the world than to have both money and status without Jesus (Luke 18:18–30).

A WORD FROM JAMES

In the New Testament Wisdom Literature, the book of James teaches us that if in the midst of trials of many kinds, we find that we lack wisdom, we should ask God and he will give it to us (James 1:5). When James invites those under trial to ask for wisdom, he does not refer primarily to our need to make decisions. It is true that if we are uncertain regarding which path to take with a job, or a spouse, or a school, we can ask God for wisdom. But James has something more profound in mind.

Like the Preacher in Ecclesiastes, James likewise teaches us about folly and wisdom (what James calls two kinds of wisdom). The wisdom from below chooses bitter jealousy, selfish ambition, false boasting, lying, disorder, and every vile practice to navigate life under the sun. In contrast, the wisdom from above chooses meekness, purity, peace, gentleness, reasonableness, mercy, impartiality, and sincerity as its response to what is grievously done under the sun (James 3:13–18).

When James says to ask for wisdom when we lack it, what he means is that when in our trials we lack meekness or gentleness or reasonableness as we are trying to navigate the trauma, we are meant to ask God.

Instead of going on in our lack and trying to respond to what tests us with bitterness, lying, or vile practice, we recognize that God is present. He remains our hope for maintaining a witness to his wisdom in the trial-laden world. It is the wisdom of God that gives voice to our way of resistance and response to life as it is under the sun. Not because the world cherishes it, or because the world will praise us for it, but because it is good and right and true to the God who has covenanted with us and to whom we belong. We seek to overcome the evil that we rightly hate, not by abandoning the world to evil, or by multiplying evils, but by letting evil go and seeking to respond instead with what is good (Rom. 12:21).

It is as if the Preacher says to us: "Hate life! Join the wisdom resistance!"

CONCLUSION

"You have heard that it was said, 'You shall love your neighbor and hate your enemy,'" Jesus teaches. "But I say to you, love your enemies and pray for those who persecute you" (Matt. 5:43–44).

To say that we hate life is to say that we no longer love what the enemies of it do. It is to declare that we will no longer join in and wear such grievous clothes. Instead, we will take up the cause of the gnashing world with prayer, lament, and honest speech. We hallow the wisdom that seeks to recover love in the world.

In order for us to grow in this way, we too will need what the Preacher had. God gave the Preacher wisdom. God gave the Preacher himself. We too will have help to hate life properly and to respond wisely, if only God will give us himself and his wisdom. We look to the God that Solomon served. We too need such gracious provision. Jesus is that provision. He is our wisdom. In his laments we learn what he loves. With this, we learn that the Preacher doesn't hate people, God, or the good pleasures that God gives us. What he hates is this life because what is often done under the sun is worthy of our heaving sighs and tears.

> O Jerusalem, Jerusalem, the city that kills the prophets and stones those who are sent to it! How often would I have gathered your children together as a hen gathers her brood under her wings, and you were not willing! (Luke 13:34)

Sometimes when we look at what we cry about, we discover what we love.

QUESTIONS FOR DISCUSSION

1. What is meant by the assertion, "Every lament is a love song"? How does what you grieve about reveal positively and negatively what you love?
2. In what sense does the Preacher hate life?
3. Why is his way of hating life wise?
4. How does his way of hating life differ from what we are used to feeling or hearing? How is it possible that this kind of hatred identifies an act of faith?
5. Why be wise if doing so doesn't change life under the sun?
6. Describe how the New Testament book of James informs this teaching in Ecclesiastes?
7. How does this section of Ecclesiastes point us to Jesus?

CHAPTER SIX

DEATH AND THE JOY OF
AN ORDINARY LIFE

Let not Ambition mock their useful toil,
Their homely joys, and destiny obscure;
Nor Grandeur hear with a disdainful smile
The short and simple annals of the Poor.[1]

What would we do if we knew that the shelves of our days were nearly empty and that death was soon? In response to a question of this kind, the Reformer Martin Luther allegedly gave an answer. "If I knew that tomorrow the world would go to pieces," he said, "I would still plant my apple tree."

Whether this anecdote represents a bit of lore or a true account of something Luther actually said, the sentiment well captures what the Preacher seems to have in mind here. He has told us thus far that life and its pleasures have no ultimate gain in them. Good pleasures are like watermelons used to play soccer. They are good in themselves but will splatter if we try to use them to score a goal. He has also taught us that even the wise have no immunity to the miseries under the sun and that they too are going to die. The Preacher then taught us to raise our protest from the vantage point of our regard for God by wisely hating these facts under the sun. So, what now?

In essence, now he tells us, death is coming, so we must learn from God to plant our apple trees.

In Ecclesiastes 2, for example, the Preacher brings death to the forefront. "How the wise dies just like the fool!" (Eccl. 2:16). Then, in light of our impending death amid the gainless pleasures of this world, the Preacher tells us what we should do. "There is nothing better for a person than that he should eat and drink and find enjoyment in his toil" (Eccl. 2:24). In fact, he now tells us that the power to enjoy these ordinary human things like food, drink, and our works under the sun is a gift from God (Eccl. 2:25).

Likewise, in Ecclesiastes 9, the Preacher invites us to swim in these same waters. He dives and splashes into death and Sheol. He treads these waters where his feet cannot touch bottom. "This is the place to which we are all going," he heaves (see Eccl. 9:10). From beyond the shallows, he shouts from the deeps to us:

> Go, eat your bread in joy, and drink your wine with a merry heart, for God has already approved of what you do. Let your garments be always white. Let not oil be lacking on your head. Enjoy life with the wife whom you love, all the days of your vain life that he has given you under the sun, because this is your portion in life and in your toil at which you toil under the sun. Whatever your hand finds to do, do it with your might. (Eccl. 9:7–10)

Moreover, in Ecclesiastes 12, the Preacher writes a poem about aging (Eccl. 12:1–7). As we move from youth to old age, we accumulate experiences with evil days. "I have no pleasure in them," we will say (Eccl. 12:1). And the day will come, when "the mourners go about the streets" because "a man is going to his eternal home" (Eccl. 12:5). When the day of death comes, men of strength weaken, women of song "are brought low" (Eccl. 12:4), fears and vulnerabilities rise, flowers, birds, and grasshoppers seem to fade from their task and from our view, and every ordinary tool or craft that we used to get through our ordinary days remains, though we do not. "The dust returns to the earth as it was, and the spirit returns to God who gave it" (Eccl. 12:7). In light of this coming day of our funeral, what do we do? Rejoice, remove, and remember (Eccl. 11:8–10). We learn to rejoice in our youth but also in every day that we get to live.

We remove vexation from our hearts and we walk in the ways our hearts desire. We are free to pursue the good desires we possess. In this rejoicing and removing, we remember our Creator, we remember the dark days, we remember our desires, we remember that he will judge us, that he will give us joy and bring us ultimately home.

In fact, the Preacher repeats and therefore reinforces this teaching of ordinary joys in response to death and the vanity under the sun.

> I perceived that there is nothing better for them than to be joyful and to do good as long as they live; also that everyone should eat and drink and take pleasure in all his toil—this is God's gift to man. (Eccl. 3:12–13)

> So I saw that there is nothing better than that a man should rejoice in his work, for that is his lot. (Eccl. 3:22)

> Behold, what I have seen to be good and fitting is to eat and drink and find enjoyment in all the toil with which one toils under the sun the few days of his life that God has given him, for this is his lot. Everyone also to whom God has given wealth and possessions and power to enjoy them, and to accept his lot and rejoice in his toil—this is the gift of God. For he will not much remember the days of his life

because God keeps him occupied with joy in his heart. (Eccl. 5:18–20)

THE PREACHER AND OUR NEIGHBORS

The Preacher's response to death likely surprises us. Other ways of responding to death might seem more appropriate.

For example, some of our neighbors under the sun will say that despair offers the only reasonable response to this emptiness and death. We become like Eeyore in the famed *Winnie-the-Pooh* stories. This donkey has lost his tail. He lives in "Eeyore's Gloomy Place: Rather Boggy and Sad." The place is made of sticks. The sticks regularly collapse. He builds them again only for them to collapse again. We might expect the Preacher to shout at God, "Everything I put together, you tear down! There is no point!" Or he might pronounce that God is dead and that meaning has died with him. Such nihilistic neighbors don't look at death and plant an apple tree. Instead, these neighbors sit down beside the tree and weep, waiting for death to come, or hastening it for both them and the tree, or mocking or shouting at everyone who passes by, that nothing matters, that morality is made-up, and that no future exists.

Other neighbors become cynical but not despairing. They see through the irrelevance of those who strive after the world's fames, riches, and works. Appearances are trite. Meaning is a fiction and our lives are nothing more than a story that we tell ourselves. "But hey," they seem to say, "there are still basic things worth enjoying like food and sleep and nature." "Why not marvel at the sunset while we can see it?" The cynic's advice is that "we stop distracting ourselves with accomplishments, accept the meaningless-ness of the universe, lie down on a park bench and get some sun while we have the chance."[2] This neighbor rests in the shade of the apple tree. Unshaven and unbathed, he watches you and shakes his head at your pretensions and the emptiness for which you wear yourself out. He folds his hands, enjoys the shade, and eats the fruit as long as it lasts.

The meaningless life leads still other neighbors to identify joy with self-indulgence and to make pleasuring ourselves the goal of our vain lives. This neighbor will cut down the tree, make a fire, cook the fruit, invite friends over, and party all night with each other, shouting, "Let's eat, drink, and be merry for tomorrow we die!" (see 1 Cor. 15:32). "Pleasures do not satisfy forever, but forever doesn't exist so who cares?" Plenty of pleasures are waiting in line to make you feel good tonight, the next night, and the next, on and on until you die. What could be better? Take what you want and indulge yourself!

But in Oscar Wilde's *The Picture of Dorian Gray*, "this new spirituality" of hedonism provides lifelong pleasures to a man while leaving his soul dark and empty still. For our "mad hungers" do not feel full, but rather they grow more ravenous as we feed them. Feeding our senses thrills us but cannot cure what aches us.[3]

Sometimes hedonism takes a more obviously horrid turn. In Flannery O'Connor's haunting short story, a serial killer tells his hedonistic perspective to a family while he kills them one by one. He philosophizes about how in the absence of a real Savior or meaning there is "nothing for you to do but enjoy the few minutes you got left the best way you can—by killing somebody or burning down his house or doing some other meanness to him. No pleasure but meanness," he says.[4] The trigger pulls, the living die, and he smiles. Such neighbors respond to the vanity under the sun by hacking the tree down, carving branches into spears, and hurling these and the apples to bruise their neighbors for a laugh.

In this context of nihilism, cynicism, and hedonism, Christians often choose pietism or escapism[5] as their way of dealing with all of it under the sun. At its worst, the pietist pays no attention to the apple tree and leaves it to decay. He or she runs to her closet to pray instead. Death is coming. Eternal matters are in the balance. Attention to the physical and bodily is waste. The condition of our soul is all that matters now.

The escapist on the other hand romanticizes the vanity under the sun and puts slogans to it. Things really aren't that bad. Pain isn't warranted. Tears aren't faithful. Everything is neat and tidy under the sun. God doesn't make ugly. Just believe. The tree and your soul will both be fine. Don't fret yourself with such questions. God wouldn't want us to concern ourselves too much with such things. Spiritual jargon and nice songs are used to distract us from the wise hatred we are meant to learn.

The simple believes everything, but the prudent gives thought to his steps. (Prov. 14:15)

The prudent sees danger and hides himself, but the simple go on and suffer for it. (Prov. 22:3)

Powerfully, the Preacher differs from each of these responses. He agrees with the nihilist that meaning is lost with us. But he maintains that God exists and is knowable. Therefore purpose can be recovered, not beneath the sun, but in the One who created the sun.

The Preacher likewise agrees with the cynic that much of what we aspire to in life is nothing more than "striving after wind" and distraction. Ordinary enjoyments such as food, shelter, and nature are enough for us. We possess within them a certain kind of pleasantness. Yet, relation to God and to our neighbors for his sake remains. This will require more than our mockery and life-long vacation from the world. There is a sadness we are meant to enter, a recovery of beauty that we are meant to long for, neighbors we are meant to stand with and love.

Likewise, Ecclesiastes does not travel with hedonism. Though our senses are gifts and pleasures bring delight, the Preacher insists that there remains a difference between lust and love, between grateful receiving and greedy consuming, between sacred regard and selfish use. Self-indulgence implies that love is not required; that we need care nothing for patience, restraint, humility, and the protection of others from being treated as our property or our toys.

Furthermore, beyond the grave, the Preacher maintains that there is more than an empty nothing or amnesia that awaits us. We have a future relationship with the One who created us, including his judgment for our treatment of him and others while we lived under the sun, and granting the final vindication of God and the purpose for which he created us (Eccl. 3:17).

Consequently, the Preacher also challenges escapist "Christian" responses to the world. Our impending death calls us to prayer and piety (Eccl. 5) but not in isolation from the physical provisions of God for us. Our spouses, our food, our place, our work, and our enjoyment of each are not meant to fade from view when death speaks. Rather, the Preacher teaches us that these provisions are meant to take their place center stage in our lives with God. These are his gifts to us and are not trash to be thrown into the dumpster while we carry our Bibles and sit in the alley, waiting with praise and prayer for death to come.

And those who mail "don't worry, be happy" fliers to the addresses of the mad, the tempted, the lost, and the murdered will find no resonance with this man of God who wisely hollers, "I hate this life. What is done under the sun is grievous!" While the sloganeers create their Christian fortune cookies with one-sentence inspirations, the wise sit with the recipients of those fortunes and grieve with them at their tables as they grapple with the inability of such jargon to recover the Eden that we've lost, the satisfaction that our hearts pine for, or the lost nobility for which our life under the sun was made.

In sum, death has pointed its headlights at us and started its engine. Therefore, we must learn from God how to enjoy what he has given to us, knowing that none of it can save or satisfy us. Trying to turn a grapefruit into a baseball doesn't dismiss the value of the grapefruit, but it makes for a disappointing baseball game. If we want to enjoy the fruit's value, we have to treat it according to the use God gave it and resist trying to use it for things it was not made for. A grapefruit cannot give us the thrill of a home run, but it can make a breakfast pleasant.

So it is with our spouses, our food, our work, and our place in the world. Neither of these can satisfy our souls or provide the gain that only God can give. Trying to use them as such will only disappoint us. Yet, these creations are God-given and possess divine purpose. A joy resides within them for our notice and this by his design. We are meant to taste these joys for which God's gifts were made. How do we learn these tastes?

PRACTICING HIS PRESENCE

To begin looking at death, the Preacher recovers our sense of God in all ordinary things. "This" (by which he means, our lot and our toil) "is the gift of God" (Eccl. 3:13; 5:19).

A gift isn't earned, it is given. When someone gives us a gift, we do not purchase it, we receive it. A gift is not deserved or obligated; it is bestowed out of the kindness and desire of the giver. We are prone to complain about the gifts someone gives us. Entitlement, discontentment, and ingratitude cause us publicly to mock it or to attempt to return it privately for something more desirable. But the Preacher reorients us. To taste the sweetness of ordinary joys, we learn to enter each day with a conviction about the givenness of all things. The Western idea that we should "seize the day" would change from "get out there, assert yourself, take it, make it happen" to something more like "open your hands, pay attention to what God is giving and what he is not, receive with humility what he gives as enough, thankfully pursue this, enjoy this."

In the classic writing, *The Practice of the Presence of God*, Brother Lawrence captures this point. Lawrence disliked working in the kitchen in which he worked daily for fifteen years. But he learned from God's grace how to rejoice among the pots, pans, and water-wrinkled hands at "doing little things for the love of God." He would have preferred to change jobs and do something larger and more seemingly meaningful, but he was stuck. Over time, however, he noticed that maybe, "sanctification does not depend so much on changing our activities as it does on doing them for God rather than for ourselves." For this reason, grace began to teach him that the most effective way of communicating with God was simply to do the work set before him. "Our actions should unite us to God when we are in our daily activities," he began to say, "just as our prayers unite us to him in our private devotions."[6]

Standing on the porch confronting the reality of death under the scorching sun we cry out, "Where is God?" The Preacher answers our cry. "Under the sun, God is found right where you are waiting amid the ordinary things of your daily life. Your lot is his gift."

A *lot* was like a straw that people chose out of one's hand when making decisions. The size of the straw (lot) that one was given determined their role or place in how the decision being made was carried out. To say "this is one's lot" is similar to some in my time who refer to dealing cards and playing with "the hand that one is dealt."

But, in this case, when the Preacher says "this is his lot," he does not highlight our miserable circumstances under the sun. He has already done this. So now, he takes our eyes off of all of those difficulties and asks us to look instead at "our lot" or "portion," the fact that the life of every human being consists mainly in this: we've been given a place to be, some things to do, a need for sustenance, and a people to share this with. God originates these gifts. God is present with his gifts.

"By thanksgiving we duly celebrate his kindnesses toward us ascribing to his liberality every blessing that enters into our lot."[7] Though death exists. So do apple trees.

In this light, the Preacher tells us about two different kinds of people under the sun. The first one is learning to see each aspect of his lot as a gift that indicates God's good character and active presence toward him. God visits with him in his ordinary toil. God "keeps him occupied with joy in his heart" (Eccl. 5:20) with these visits. It is as if God shares his delight with the man and he too finds this delight in the ordinary.

In contrast, the second kind of person has his lot but does not see God in it. This one uses what he has and makes his life with it, but he derives no present empowerment from God to enjoy what he has as God does (Eccl. 6:2). His is a godless happiness in his lot. God's gift is not recognized. God's presence is not sought in the gift. And the joy that God has in this shared attention together does not take place. This is doubly sad. Not only is this second person's life under the sun fraught with miseries worth wisely hating, this person also derives no sense of God or of God's joy from the ordinary gifts of his marriage, his food, his work, his dwelling place, or his possessions.

Therefore, the power to "accept" our lot (Eccl. 5:19) does not refer to numb resignation or pointless apathy. Nor is the Preacher simply telling us that "death is coming, therefore stop and smell the roses while you can." Acceptance rather involves our alertness to God's presence among the gifts he has given us and the sense of his joy that he intends to provide us through our visiting with him among them under the sun.

If the Preacher cries out with hatred and says, "Where can I find God?" he seems to answer, "God is where you are! Find him, not in what you do not have, but amid the smallest things that remain, he will find you! The grief under the sun can only eclipse our views of God, but they cannot stop his light." His gifts, however small, won't quit even amid the pillaging of war-torn once-Eden. For this reason, Corrie Ten Boom speaks of grateful joy with God amid the horrid tortures of her concentration camp. She and her sister learned to give thanks for the fleas they had. The guards wouldn't go to the flea-infested place. But God would. He met with them there. Confoundedly, they tenaciously gave thanks to him as they relished each other in that hellish place.[8]

Therefore, "acceptance," by being kept occupied by the joys of God in our lot amid the brutality of life under the sun, leads us to cultivate a "moment-by-moment" way of living as we seek to live in the reality of his presence. Admittedly, "the practical problem for us individually is to find a point at which we begin to live moment by moment in reality."[9] However, the problem isn't that we don't talk about living moment by moment. Many people do.

The nihilist seeks to live moment by moment in order to rehearse the emptiness of it all.

The cynic seeks to live moment by moment in order to mock the pretenses we chase.

The hedonist seeks to live moment by moment in order to limit pain and to secure good sensations.

The Christian escapist seeks to live moment by moment in order to secure removal from the physical and the ugly.

The problem then is the kind of moment-by-moment awareness that we need the grace to cultivate. The Preacher invites us to see each moment as the means by which God pursues us among the pots and pans and marriage kisses of our lot. To accept this as our reality is to pursue God's visitation right where we find ourselves. Each minute contains a sanctuary for worship; each hour offers a kitchen table for conversation with him; each day is a wood path for walking with him; each moment, no matter how wonderfully ordinary or flea-infested, offers enough for intimacy with him.

Jesus sought the Father in his boyhood days (Luke 2:49). When Jesus broke bread for a meal (Luke 24:30) or when he had nothing to eat (John 4:31–33), he saw either circumstance in relation to the presence of the Father. Whether Jesus was alone (Luke 5:16) or joyful with his friends (Luke 10:21) or abandoned by them (Luke 22:39–46) or when enemies mistreated him (John 18:33–36), Jesus discerned the presence of the Father in those moments. Even on the cross, with the violence from under the sun heaping upon him, Jesus sought the communion of the Father (Luke 23:34, 46). Jesus lives what the Preacher in Ecclesiastes teaches. Jesus will take our moment-by-moment attempts at godless happiness upon himself. He will purchase for us the moment-by-moment relationship with the Father that he lived to fulfill all wisdom.

GETTING BACK TO HUMAN BASICS

In the original Chicken Little story, Chicken Little is hit by an acorn on his beak and he feels the bruise. He thinks the acorn is the sky. Fear seizes him. "The sky is falling!" he yells. So he tries to enlist everyone to help him, eventually enlisting Foxy Loxy for aid in stopping the sky from falling. Foxy Loxy eventually eats Chicken Little for dinner. Among the many versions of this story through the generations, the two main themes are these. One, some of us need to learn, that just because an acorn falls on our beak and we feel its bruise, this doesn't mean that all is lost. Two, some forms of help are no help at all. In fact, some things will harm us in help's name.

The Preacher has been walking us through the dark creepy basement of the fallen world with his flashlight. It would seem that if anybody could come to the conclusion that the sky is falling, it would be the Preacher. But the Preacher doesn't panic. He hates it. He grieves it. He declares it ruthless and ugly and empty. But he refuses to run toward the welcoming arms of the nihilist, the cynic, the hedonist, or the religious escapist. That kind of help doesn't.

Instead, the Preacher believes that God has not left the mess but remains here in it and with us. In that light, we start with what we have and we do this little bit each day with God. But how?

To begin, we eat our bread and drink our wine because "God already has approved what you do" (Eccl. 9:7). Some of us are wondering what God's will is for our lives. Among all the things we do not know, we start with what we do know. It's Saturday morning; we wake up; whatever choice we make for how to use the day makes our tender conscience restless and guilt ridden with a sense of wrong or waste. The Preacher frees us. When it comes to our tending our lot with our spouse and family, our work, our food, and our place, God has already told us that he approves of this use of time. When Adam and Eve loved each other, cultivated the garden, took time for meals, and cared for the place with God, it was enough in God's eyes.

My toddler son would always ask if he could get a cup of water. "You never have to ask if you want water," I'd say. "You can just go ahead and drink it." Similarly, we needn't wonder if God approves of our paying attention to our little portion and our ordinary lot with him. We needn't ask if he approves.

"But we are all going to die!" we counter. "I know, make a sandwich, cook a fish," the Preacher responds. "But the sky is falling!" we shout. "I know, have some tea, enjoy this wine with me," he says. "God is here."

"But everything is meaningless!" I know, go ahead and wash your clothes. "But injustice racks the broken world!" I know, go ahead and take a bath or clean your face when you can. "Let your garments be always white. Let not oil be lacking on your head" (Eccl. 9:8). "God hasn't quit."

"But what do you mean? Nothing satisfies us! It's all vanity!" I know, listen to your wife's voice, hold her hand, wash the dishes together, plan your life, learn to make wondrous love, work redemptively through your pains together, help the kids, do not deny how much you love her, embrace this. "But death is coming!" I know; "enjoy life with the wife whom you love" (Eccl. 9:9). "God is here."

"But wisdom gets us no favors here!" Yes, so go ahead and start your day. "But life isn't fair!" I know. The grief is terrible. But try to do what you love as you are able. Do it passionately with all of your heart even if you are stuck doing some work that is beneath your dreams. Still, God can meet you there. "Whatever your hand finds to do, do it with your might" (Eccl. 9:10).

Adam and Eve had nothing more than this. Their lot was God's gift. They had each other, the place, a bit of work, and food, and they had God. Death came. But this original provision for which the human heart was made, remains.

My grandpa and grandma on my Dad's side live in Camden, Tennessee. This little country town isn't far from the town of Bucksnort. In that unknown place, they make a life, including expressing their love for Jesus through a little local church. In their mid- to late eighties, I spoke to them on the telephone. They had just gone fishing and were cleaning the twenty-six fish they caught that day.

"How are you doing?" I asked my grandpa.

"Well, we got up this morning. It was a good day," he said lightly but seriously. Maybe my nervous laugh and then my quiet caused him to feel that he should explain what he meant.

"Zack, when your grandmother and I wake up, we give thanks to God, because at our age, waking up is not a promise. Then, if we have the strength to do what we had planned to do that day, we give thanks to God that we had the strength to do it; because at our age, strength and health comes and goes. If we get a nap in and we wake up, we give thanks. If it's dinnertime and we're sitting down to eat, we give thanks not only for our food, but also that we can eat it, and that we made it through the day that far. After that, when we go to bed at night, we look at each other and then back on the day and we thank God for another day that he gave us to live. So, today we went fishing, and what do you know, we have all of these fish! The Good Lord must still have a purpose for us."

Eden was our purpose. Trying to bust out of it remains our constant downfall. God and his joys are found here within our lot and not somewhere else. After all, once we get somewhere else, we will have to face the same questions once gainless boredom or restless discontent takes hold of us there too. Sooner or later, whether due to age, sickness, or circumstance, there will be no other place to go, no other work to try, no other wife to leave, and no other menu from which we can order. At some point, we all have to come to terms with the spiritual truth that true joy is found in God and God is found right where His gifts are. God's gifts are our lot. This means that right here where we are is where God will be found no matter what ruckus death makes.

THE PRAYER AND PROTEST
OF ORDINARY THINGS

A toddler asks an important man (who also happens to be the toddler's dad) to go to the park. The important man has important things on his important mind. Riding a bike to the park, sliding down slides, playing tag beneath the monkey bars and playfully soaking their heads with a water fountain, and getting food together seem like a waste of important time. The important man either does not take the time or he does so unhappily out of obligation, his mind elsewhere, and no sense of God for the moment of his lot.

But the Preacher's words are a gracious provision from God for the important man. The important man begins to pray for seemingly unimportant things. He prays that God would empower him to slide on a slide, to play tag, to listen and hear his son, and to splash fountain water on each other. The grace of wisdom begins to open all of the windows in his life. Every little thing in his lot is becoming a means of potential joy and fellowship that God can give amid the stresses and frustrations under the sun. His wife, his work, his food, his place all become something to pray for the empowerment of God's joy in them.

Consequently, when someone walks into his house, he provides them food and drink, less and less for appearances or approval, and more and more because food and drink were meant for human joy in God. He sits at his table with guests and learns by grace of wisdom to say amid the harming things that still screech out in the world, "This is good and is no waste!" Such Edenic moments signify our protest to life as it is under the sun. The Preacher has already implied the emptiness of gluttony by his exposure of gainless pleasures. But on the other hand, those of us who see eating as a waste of time or who see famine as something to ignore are missing God in these moments.

Similarly, the rich are prone to clean and dress for appearances' sake in order to secure their places in the world. The cynic rightly mocks this from the apple tree's shade. But the cynic's unshowered stench on purpose wrongly mocks the poor. The poor have few garments. The war-torn have little time to wash. To bathe rightly is to take a stand in the world. Amid all of the indignities done to the human being, we will take up our bit of soap and quietly protest that a human life wasn't made to be spat on.

Likewise, somewhere along the line, men and women look beyond their wives or their husbands in order to find the gain they long for. Others passively fade away always in the house but never actually present toward the other. Still others use fists and threats as substitutes for care and companionship. These do not realize that no matter who they pledge their lives to, the questions will remain the same. Can they learn to discern God here in ordinary covenant love and to taste the joy he has for them right where they are, such as they are? Only God's provision can do it!

The grace of his wisdom teaches us to give ourselves to our portion of work, food, marriage, family, and a bath, because these things are what God gave for human flourishing. Eden has changed. But this purpose for us has not.

JESUS AND OUR LOT

When Jesus came to redeem us, he did so, not by bypassing the ordinary human lot in life, but by recovering it. He was born in a stable, with parents in a town. He worked with wood, in a trade, for a local community for thirty years. He had brothers and sisters, a community, and friendships. His ministry provided food for the hungry, bodily recovery for the sick, drink for the wedding feast, restoration to a right mind, and the recovery of relationships, married and otherwise. His many meetings with ordinary people occurred in homes or in local synagogues or markets or at feasts. When Jesus healed people or forgave them, these restored ones did not escape their lot in life but they returned to it.

Peter's mother-in-law was healed. The result? She showed hospitality as a host (Matt. 8:14–15). Lazarus was raised from the dead but received no immunity in this life. He ate with his friends while his enemies sent him death threats (John 12:10). The man who was demon possessed with the broken brain was put into his right mind. The result? Jesus sent him back home to follow him among his friends and family (Mark 5:19). In fact, Jesus describes the results of his healing work.

The blind receive their sight and the lame walk, lepers are cleansed and the deaf hear, and the dead are raised up, and the poor have good news preached to them. (Matt. 11:5)

Now these human beings can see what is under the sun or walk within it or hear its sounds in the town where they live among the people of their community while Rome still occupies them. The meaninglessness of toil without gain abounds.

When Jesus rose from the grave, among the first things that he did was to invite his friends to catch fish, cook it, and eat together by the sea with a fire on a beach. And all of this while death is coming, the world needs saving, Herod and Pontius Pilate are doing their worst, and life under the sun remains cruel.

What is it that we believe God is trying to do for us by sending his Son? Just as the Preacher foreshadows by his wisdom, Jesus did not come to give us an escape from our lot, misuse our lot, or make our lot our god. Jesus cut wood, ate food, lived in a family, and had a hometown. He forgave and healed people so that they could learn in him how to do the same as God intended. When Adam and Eve left Eden, they were not given a different calling. Their calling remained as it was even though death was now alive in the world. They were to love each other, work, care for the place, and meet with God. The calling didn't change. The environment did.

This is why the Preacher, while he describes how difficult this environment has become, still upholds the old Edenic calling as our way of life and joy. This is why the New Testament letters teach us in Jesus how to live where we do in Christ, so that our marriages, our parenting, our work, our possessions, and our neighbors are relearned in the Lord. Even heaven itself, according to Jesus, is like a wedding feast or a great banquet or a place with many mansions. We will gather there in that place, with work to do, with each other, in the presence of God. The under-the-sun tears and miseries and death will finally die. The environment will finally return. Our lot will once again reunite with the context that suits it.

CONCLUSION

A story tells us about criminals paying for their crimes within a prison of cruel mistreatment.

Year after year in this prison one man says to another, "I played a mean harmonica as a young man. Lost interest in it though. Didn't make much sense in here."

The other man responds, "Here is where it makes the most sense. You need to play it so that you don't forget."

"Forget what?" asks the first man.

"Forget that there are places in this world that aren't made out of stone, that there is something inside that these stone walls cannot take away."

"What are you talking about?" the first man retorts.

"Hope," the other man answers. "It is the wonder of wonders."[10]

The Preacher tells us, "Death is coming!" "Everything is meaningless!" "What is done under the sun is grievous and warrants our wise hatred!"

Yet, there exists a place of joy that the cruel walls cannot take away. That place is our lot. Our lot offers hope under the sun. Death is here, but God is here too. Death will die. But God is Immanuel, "God with us."

QUESTIONS FOR DISCUSSION

1. What do you think about Martin Luther's alleged answer when asked about what he would do if he knew death was around the corner? How would you answer this question?
2. How does the Preacher's answer to this question surprise you?

3. Describe your reactions to the idea of practicing the presence of God in the ordinary. Reflect on the story of the fleas.

4. Which voice do you most resemble? Most dislike? The nihilist, the cynic, the hedonist, or the Christian escapist? Put in your own words how the Preacher's message differs from these others.

5. What about your lot bores you, annoys you, or pains you right now? What about your lot is beautiful and good?

6. How does acceptance differ from resignation? What do you need from Jesus in order for him to recover your acceptance of him in the ordinary of your life?

CHAPTER SEVEN

KNOWING THE TIMES

*"One must summer and winter with the land
and wait its occasions."*[1]

I bought a book called something like *Missouri Gardening, a Month-by-Month Guide.* In light of the Missouri seasons, the book breaks down what to do each month of the year in order to tend the trees, grasses, flowers, soils, and gardens that we care for. In the winter when the grass hibernates from growth and the lawnmower sits on vacation in the barn or garage, the book says, use this time to maintain the lawnmower. I might not feel like removing old gas from the tank, or oil from its container, but to leave the mower in such a condition lessens the likelihood that it will start when I need it to come spring, when the grass and the honeysuckle are tired of being tired and decide to renew their zeal for making themselves known.

I know what the book says from experience. Stubborn, I wanted to use time my own way and throw off having to follow its moods. So, I left that old gas in there through the winter, only to find that spring unexpectedly sprinted to a start and left me knee-deep in grass with a mower that couldn't ignite. Lawnmowers are like people. If we skip what we need in the season given, we don't start so well when the season changes and its demands are made. We make a rough time of it—trying to work in one season without receiving the care and mentoring that a different season was designed to give but didn't. Some of us are always trying to "pluck up what is planted," because we ourselves never learned what it meant to surrender to "a time to plant" (Eccl. 3:2). Life isn't timeless. The times limit our choices and require others of us. The lot we've been given cannot flourish without attention to the seasons that roll through.

Therefore, a season designates a beginning and an end in which weathers, landscapes, climates, and creatures experience changes that will require adjustment to the conditions. We wear coats in winter, but the summer frees us to leave our sweaters indoors. The red cardinal sits in trees and sings in my April yard. But December frightens the leaves to death and few redbirds will brave the frosted branches, which the winter makes bare and cold.

To make this point, the Preacher wants us to imagine for a moment that we are like farmers who must learn how to deal with the occasions that regularly cycle through a year. By using the word *seasons* (Eccl. 3:1) he puts the sands of our times within the larger mountains and skies of God's creation. God "made the moon to mark the seasons; the sun knows its time for setting" (Ps. 104:19). In fact, "while the earth remains, seedtime and harvest, cold and heat, summer and winter, day and night, shall not cease" (Gen. 8:22). Time offers a repeated rhythm of beginnings and endings. Learning to receive rather than resist these rhythms, we draw nearer to God and his purposes for the life and lot he has given us. In short, we enter an already established routine that we did not choose but that shapes how we live.

So, a farmer has to learn to recognize, submit to, and plan accordingly for the seasons that rotate through their corner of land year upon year. For example, there are times of the year in which the weather and soil conditions are ripe for a tree to bear its fruit (Ps. 1:3). There are also times of the year in which no fruit will come no matter what we do (Mark 11:13). An unwillingness to recognize

118

and surrender to what time it is within the season that attends us can harm a farmer.

> He who gathers in summer is a prudent son, but he who sleeps in harvest is a son who brings shame. (Prov. 10:5)

> The sluggard does not plow in the autumn; he will seek at harvest and have nothing. (Prov. 20:4)

Therefore, sages like this Preacher teach that the wise farmer is like the ant that "prepares her bread in summer and gathers her food in harvest" (Prov. 6:8). The point is this. In order to have the sustenance his family needs, the farmer has to learn how to humbly surrender to what the time requires when the time requires it. He may think, feel, or desire otherwise, but the planting season comes and goes, and the plow won't move without the farmer's hand.

Farmer Wendell Berry recounts a conversation on this theme with his wife Tanya.

> After we planted a garden last Tuesday, Tanya spoke of how much she liked the idea that we had done it, not because of any convention or custom or law, but because it was time.[2]

The times are marked out for us and we learn from God what we need to do to tend our lot when they arrive.

THE DISQUIET AND THE DELIGHT

The Preacher identifies two basic kinds of seasons or times in which we will tend our lots—disquiets and delights.

For those prone to draw the world only in pastels and who see God's purpose and nearness only in terms of smiles and victories, the Preacher boldly identifies disquieting times.

These disquieting things traumatize human beings and, as with Job, can wreak havoc on our portion in life and our attempts to discern God's moment-by-moment joy in our lot.

A time to die	A time to refrain from embracing
A time to pluck up what is planted	A time to lose
A time to kill	A time to cast away
A time to break down	A time to tear
A time to weep	A time to be silent
A time to mourn	A time for war

For those who want to falsely relieve the tension on the other side, who describe the world only with pain and who see the world only in terms of its mud, the Preacher counters by describing the delightful things. These inspire and nurture hope in our lots as we handle the times within God's purpose and nearness.

A time to be born	A time to embrace
A time to plant	A time to seek
A time to heal	A time to keep
A time to build up	A time to sew
A time to laugh	A time to speak
A time to dance	A time to love
A time to gather stones together	A time for peace

It is as if the Preacher says to us, "As you travel out there in the world, under the sun, remember this about

120

your times! There are beginnings and endings, goods and evils, things we choose and choices that we did not make but must deal with. We age, we face realities with relationships and necessities with work. We encounter varying human moods and actions. Such occasions await all of us."

UNPREPARED AND FRAGMENTED

In all of this, the Preacher brings up subjects and times that exist under the sun that we'd rather not think about. Some of us would rather not think about what is delightful. Others of us avoid what is disquieting. The Preacher intends to mentor us into a way of being human before God that has a capacity to honestly recognize what is there and the grace to look to God for it and within it no matter what it is. As we notice what aspects of life we tend to avoid, we will see the disquiets and the delights that we are yet unprepared to handle.

Theologically unprepared, we can believe that if we or someone we love experiences one of these disquieting things, then God has singled us out, made an exception out of us, and he does not love us. Likewise, if we experience a delightful occasion, we can believe that God is bringing us favorably into his "clique" or on the other hand, tricking us, baiting us, and setting us up for a fall.

Relationally unprepared, we can believe that if someone experiences one of these disquieting or delightful things, the reason must arise from something they have personally done to deserve it or to bring it on. Either way, we can self-righteously judge the first and secretly covet or envy the second. Sadly, we will not know how to think truly about God or to walk relationally with neighbors or family members if we, or they, experience times that we have committed our whole lives to avoiding. Consequently, we often hurt those who must walk through what we'd prefer not to think about.

Likewise, our friends and family can mishandle us. When we experience a circumstance under the sun that they sought to avoid all of their lives, they sting us with their theological and relational unpreparedness. They underestimate and mismanage what such times actually require of us. Yesterday the leg bones broke. Today, hunched on crutches we turtle and snail along. Rather than slow down or ice the swelling with us, they run on ahead shouting back to us with cheerleading voices that the brisk walk or the long jog will do us some good.

By naming the times in this way, as he did when he named the pleasures for us, the Preacher follows the sage practice of preparing people ahead of time for what can await them in the world. In fact, this act of naming and preparing reveals a long-standing practice in the Bible.

For example, in the garden of Eden, God told Adam and Eve ahead of time what they could expect regarding the landscape of their days. He told them about the land, the animals, their love for each other, their food, work, and the absence of any need to lock their doors at night. He also told them of two trees, two kinds of life, and the possibility of death should one of these trees experience misuse by them. Then, after the death came, God prepared them ahead of time regarding how their days east of Eden would change (Gen. 3:16–19).

Throughout history, the God this Preacher believes in spoke through his prophets to tell his people ahead of time what they can expect to encounter under the sun and how, in that light, to navigate it. The Wisdom Literature, such as Proverbs, describes the kinds of neighbors and qualities of circumstances ahead of time so that the young can learn prior to facing them.

Jesus, the one to whom every prophet and sage points, continued this practice.

See, I told you beforehand. (Matt. 24:25)

I have told you all things beforehand. (Mark 13:23)

And now I have told you before it takes place, so that when it does take place you may believe. (John 14:29)

As God's spokesman following God's method, it is as if the Preacher has gone ahead of us and scouted out the land and its inhabitants under the sun. He has returned from there and now proposes to share with us what he has seen regarding the kinds of times that await us under the sun.

In addition, the Preacher shows us an intermixed human expressiveness. By intermixed, I mean that the frustration and lament of disquieting times share space with the gladness and gratitude of delightful times. So, the Preacher can sound like his wisdom predecessor, Job, who wailed and groaned in the midst of unexplained misery, amid the presence of God's silence and the absence of a friend's love. Yet, through tears, Job cried out in hope.

For I know that my Redeemer lives,
    and at the last he will stand upon the earth.
And after my skin has been thus destroyed,
    yet in my flesh I shall see God. (Job 19:25–26)

The Preacher therefore resonates with the Wise One whom he himself imperfectly foreshadows. Jesus is the intermixed "man of sorrows" (Isa. 53) who gives his joy to his people (John 15:11). From the brutality and blood of the cross of violence, moaning in agony, Jesus will shout nonetheless that God and forgiveness have not died, but live, as he too will.

Time, in God's hands, graciously apprentices us toward an inward merging of our being. We do not know if the Preacher knew this about himself. If the Preacher is indeed Solomon, then perhaps such intermixture came only as the fruit of healing what he so terribly broke in his life.

But we, who hear him preach to us, clearly notice the merge. Like the apostle Paul whom Jesus changed, we too seek this apprenticeship that resists fragmentation.

Gradually, we who follow the one greater than Solomon become "as sorrowful, yet always rejoicing; as poor, yet making many rich; as having nothing, yet possessing everything" (2 Cor. 6:10). Only the wisdom of God could so transform the Preacher and give him such an emotional range and capacity. This same wisdom is now manifested fully in Jesus. In Jesus, the empowerment to defragment graciously begins its work. The Preacher highlights the mixture and the tension we are meant to embrace rather than resist.

> If a person lives many years, let him rejoice in them all; but let him remember that the days of darkness will be many. (Eccl. 11:8)

In sum, if the Preacher is our pastor, he is learning from God how to enter both what is disquieting and what is delightful with us no matter what it is. If he is our sermon giver, his sermons exalt God by uncensoring everything that our neighbors encounter and accounting for these matters as human beings who seek the purpose and nearness of God within them. If he is an apologist, he lives before us as one who is willing to think about all of life with whatever questions such disquieting and delightful times raise and to go there with us, believing that God is there already. If he is an evangelist, he bids us to look from our times to God whose purpose and nearness expose the location of our true good.

TIMES AND SEASONS

What does this mean for us?

First, to find the purpose and nearness of God, we need the grace to relate honestly toward the time dominance of life under the sun. One needn't be a follower of Jesus to know this. As one philosopher states it: "We cannot talk about our lives, ourselves, what we desire or fear, or what surrounds us, without reference to time."[3] The Preacher too recognizes this. To make this plain, the Preacher captures this constant presence of time in everything that we encounter under the sun by repeating the word twenty-eight times in eight verses and then by saying again, "there is a time for every matter and for every work" (Eccl. 3:17). Time is lungs. Without it nothing under the sun can breathe. Time forms the environment in which we live. Time is like a parent and we are its kids; it is always in our business. It is like a foreman and we are its employees; it has a say in our work and how we go about it.

Second, we need the grace therefore to relate teachably toward each day that we have been given. After all, it was God who created time (Gen. 1:14). Time with God in Eden gave space for peaceful human deciding. Time was nothing but good. Time was like a friend who allows us to spend a weekend of retreat in his home. Within this provision, we could recover and live out our purpose. Time was a living room for company, a hallway for movement, a bedroom for lovemaking and rest, a table for food, a yard for work and play, a path for reflection. Time was beautiful; a friend to humanity as both it and they co-inhabited the God-given world.

But now, time hollers at us with stress. More often than not, time haunts us, pressures us, makes us feel our shortcomings, and reveals the misuse or boredom of life. Time still gives room for human decision making, but the times in which we choose are no longer pure and the decisions we make are done as in rooms infested with creeping bugs in the rotted wood.

The Preacher picks up on this nobility and ache regarding our use of time. He reaches out to us by inviting us to think with him about it all. After all, time doesn't just happen to the religious. Each neighbor under the sun with whom we seek to relate will have something to say about time.

Some neighbors will feel that "all I have is time"; some will cherish this feeling while others will struggle to overcome boredom in order to feel useful. Other neighbors will feel awe or loss ("Where did the time go?"), or frustrated fatigue ("There aren't enough hours in the day.") or purposed urgency ("I've got to make the most of my time."), or grateful anticipation ("I've been waiting for this time to come!") or painful regret ("I wasted all of those years.") or restless waiting ("When will my time come?") or cautious fear ("I don't want this time to arrive.") or wonderful memory ("Do you remember that time that we . . . ?").

So, as a discipler, apologist, evangelist, this Preacher remembers that he too is human. He too takes up the conversation that is on his neighbors' minds. He humanly states what most of us know and can agree upon. "For everything there is a season, and a time for every matter under heaven" (Eccl. 3:1). Time is like the sky. Wherever we look, there it is. Yet, there is a problem. Humanity still has Eden in its veins. We have "eternity" in our hearts (Eccl. 3:11). Our souls instinctively yearn for a purposed life without end under this time-chained sun. The Preacher teaches us how to speak humanly and honestly about our longing for purpose, the tension we experience, and the reality of handling time with our neighbors. As those who do life with reference to the fear of the Lord, we too have these concerns in common with our neighbors.

JESUS AND APPOINTED TIMES

Time has waited long enough. God sends forth his
son (Gal. 4:4).
Herod wants to know what time the star appeared.
Infanticide follows (Matt. 2:16–17).
The time is fulfilled. Jesus comes preaching
(Mark 1:14–15).

Forty days in the wilderness. An opportune time,
the devil seeks (Luke 4:13).
The demons tremble. The dreaded time to come is
on their minds (Matt. 8:29).
Lazarus faces death. Jesus waits two days (John 11:5).
They want to arrest Jesus. But his hour has not yet
come (John 7:30).
The feast awaits. His hour is not yet (John 7:8).
The Passover arrives. Jesus announces, "My time is
at hand" (Matt. 26:18).
Jesus is betrayed. His hour has come (Mark 14:41).
They crucify him. The third hour spills his blood
(Mark 15:25).
The afternoon quits. Three hours go dark (Matt. 27:45).
The ninth hour. The Father forsakes him (Mark 15:34).
It is finished (John 19:30).
Mary weeps. Jesus waits (John 20:1–16).
Thomas doubts. Jesus waits eight days (John 20:26).
Forty days. Jesus preaches (Acts 1:3).
The day comes. Jesus ascends (Acts 1:9).
Our hour comes. Death waits. The voice of the Son
of God rises (John 5:25).
The hour comes unannounced. Prayer in Jesus ori-
ents the minutes (Mark 13:33).

Purpose, tension, and time are gathered up. One greater
than Solomon has made it so.

MAKING ADJUSTMENTS

A story is told about new soldiers in olden days who
were practicing how to shoot their rifles. One soldier stood
out from the rest. The center of the target could not escape
the keen eye and the focused sights of this combat-naive
recruit. An old veteran heard the commotion of the new
soldiers cheering. He walked over and observed the matter.

"Well done, young man," said the veteran to the recruit. "You shoot that gun real well. Now, go ahead, take another shot. I want to see it for myself."

As the young man got out his rifle, the old veteran took out his pistol. The veteran then cocked his pistol, pointed it up into the sky, and stood staring at the recruit who now felt nervous. "Load your weapon, soldier," the veteran suddenly shouted.

The new recruit fumbled with his rifle and began to load the cartridge.

"Faster!" yelled the veteran, and then he fired his pistol into the air. "*Faster!*" shouted the veteran as he pulled the trigger again.

The new recruit trembled to raise his gun into position. He tried to aim and took a frantic shot as the veteran yelled without stopping and repeatedly pulled his pistol trigger, sending booming rounds into the air. The rattled recruit missed the target completely and stood there unnerved. His young companions sat stunned and silent. The old veteran stopped yelling, put his pistol back in its holster, paused for quiet, and then looked kindly into the young recruit's eyes.

"Here in the quiet, you shoot that gun real fine. But son, where you're goin' is anything but quiet. You're gonna have to take what you can do here and learn to do it there. Until then, you ain't ready. Ain't none of you ready."

A time of quiet, distant from battle, in which one can learn among friends blesses. But there are other kinds of times in the world that are not so forgiving. In the New Testament, the apostle Peter discovered that pledging his love in the quiet would look different when the garden was intruded, the betrayer gave his kiss, and the arrests were made. Roosters can crow at times that we never would have imagined for ourselves. A person who is able to stand in one season may underestimate his ability to run that a different season can expose.

The Preacher reminds us that under the sun, the weather can change—not just the physical weather outside, but the circumstances, moods, and experiences that we may have to walk through. The Preacher sets in front of us this fact, which Job's friends forgot.

Job's friends treated Job as they would treat someone who came to a theological debate in order to philosophize about the grand questions of God and suffering. They did not adjust to the fact that Job was an actual sufferer suddenly bereft of nearly all of his portions in life. Job's friends treated Job as if they were an ecclesiastical court and Job was worthy of church discipline. They did not recognize Job's integrity hidden beneath the ugly sores. Their "time for silence" in the ashes proved much wiser and less harmful than their interpretation that it was now "a time to speak." They spoke truths out of season. They did not adjust and the damage came.

> To make an apt answer is a joy to a man, and a word *in season*, how good it is! (Prov. 15:23)

Therefore, our way of relating to God and to our neighbors will have to adjust. For example, if a spouse is experiencing a time to mourn. To treat him or her as we did when it was a time to dance and to expect the same way of relating is insensitive and unwise. Likewise, doing our work looks different during a time to build up than it does when it is a time to tear down. Church will feel different when it is a time to sew than when it is a time to tear. Prayer when it is a time to be born or to laugh will express itself differently than when it is a time to die. A time of war will change what peacetime life would have allowed but now cannot.

Because we are committed to arrange life the way we want it and to avoid what we do not prefer, many of us remain inflexible and unskilled in this wisdom of seasons. The Preacher has taught us to name these seasons without denial. Now he teaches us to yield to them and to adjust our expectations accordingly when they rotate through our lives and through the lives of our neighbors.

After all, it is nice to play outside in the yard with my family, but we cannot relate to tornado conditions the same way we would if the skies were clear and blue. To do so would harm us all. Similarly, a young man and woman, who previously enjoyed the spontaneous evenings of a different season, now have a baby. Or the teenager is no longer a toddler, and the parents collide until they recognize the season change and the adjustments that are needed. A good driver is now eighty years old, and the adult children have to ask that their parent no longer drive. The adjustment of seasons challenges old and young alike. Many of our frustrations rise from our blindness to the change of season or to the pain or joy of them, and we struggle to adjust our expectations.

The result is that we try to force others to act or the world to exist within the confines of the handful of seasons that we are most comfortable with. We try to control others to stay within the seasonal behaviors that we most prefer rather than to learn how to change and to adjust teachably, slowly, and adequately according to the grace of wisdom.

THE SEASONS AND OUR LOT

Consequently, in this context of learning how to prepare for and to adjust to the times and seasons, the Preacher again draws our attention to a resemblance of Eden: the lot that each of us has been given. He reorients our expectations back to first things.

> I perceived that there is nothing better for them than to be joyful and to do good as long as they live; also that everyone should eat and drink and take pleasure in all his toil—this is God's gift to man. (Eccl. 3:12–13)

So I saw that there is nothing better than that a man
should rejoice in his work, for that is his lot. Who can
bring him to see what will be after him? (Eccl. 3:22)

Our lot is like a ship. The seasons are like the wind
and the waves. Seasons sometimes put wind in the sails
of our lot. Other seasons toss our lot about so that it can
seem at times as if our lot is sinking and that we must
abandon ship. How do we retain our purpose of joy with
God amid the portion of food, work, family, relationships
(Eccl. 9:9), and place that he has given us when the seasons change? As we discussed earlier in this chapter, the
Preacher lists the seasons to begin Ecclesiastes 3. Let's
pause for a moment and think briefly about how these
seasons inform our lot with God.

First, in terms of our relationships, spouses, kids, and
families, we learn to discern God's nearness and purpose
for us with the births of those we love and the birth-
days that follow. Birth is joy! But there is also a time to
die. Funerals ramble through our lots. This knowledge
is enough to cause some of us to withhold love all of our
lives. We surmise that the more distance we keep the
less we hurt. Or, death surprised us. We did not know
what the Preacher teaches. We take death as something
personal to us meant by God to harm us, when in tragic
fact death forms part of the dark weather for all of us in
this once-Eden.

Relationally, we will experience times of embracing
along with the wise boundary, cautious wound, or sinful
rejection that makes each of us refrain from embracing at
times. Those who use emotional and physical distance as
a way of life are drawn out into the grace and beauty of
human touch as it was meant to be. Those who are always
touching and always familiar learn in contrast that it is
folly and not wisdom that touches every person the same.

And while it is true that the extroverted talk and the
introverted don't, both will have to come to terms with

what it means that there are times to be silent but also to speak. The extroverted have to learn that not every moment is meant for their words. Sometimes emotions and thoughts are not meant for another to consume no matter how strongly we feel or think them. The introverted, in contrast, have to learn that not every moment is meant for them to keep their thoughts to themselves. Sometimes we hurt others as much by what we leave unsaid as by what we say.

Likewise, some of us are demanding that others speak or embrace when it isn't time. Others of us are demanding silence and restraint when the time for that has actually long since passed. All of us as human neighbors speak too much or too little, and this to our pain, unless apprenticed by the grace of this wisdom which learns when to speak and when to remain present with something other than our words. Finding joy in the relational gifts of our lot means adjusting expectations and surrendering to these ways and rhythms of grace.

At this moment, some of us are ready to shout, "But how do we know when to do one and not the other?" The question is the first step away from formulaic or trite answers to make life naively manageable and toward the humility of recognizing that we will need God for each moment instead of a forced rule on which we must found our trust. Humbled, we all are meant to look to God to teach us what we ourselves do not yet have the wisdom to apply to our relationships.

Second, the work that we've been given will likewise ebb and flow in its requirements and moods during a given day, week, year, or lifetime.

A time to plant, and a time to pluck up what is planted; . . . a time to break down, and a time to build up; . . . a time to cast away stones, and a time to gather stones together; . . . a time to tear, a time to sew. (Eccl. 3:2–7)

Work has a beginning and an end. We plant but then harvest. We build but then tear down. We gather what we need but then we give it away. We sew and mend but then tear and start again.

Some of us do not know how to get started during a day when the time to start has come. We fight the planting. We hit the snooze. We have not yet learned that finding joy in our lot involves working when it is time to. Others of us do not know how to quit our work. We take it home with us. We fight Sabbaths, ignore the other relational and sustenance aspects of our lots, and retire only by making everyone around us miserable with our unrest. Joy is robbed and God seems hidden when we try to keep building what should be brought to a close or we keep trying to tear up what should be sewed back together. Our work and rest, our eager starts and our timely retirements, all have a purpose in them. They have their times in God's hands.

Third, our sustenance and material things have their time. Some of us stop looking when it is time to seek. Others throw away what was time to keep. Still others cannot let go of what time has led them to. We not only accrue, we also lose. Years after this wise Preacher, the apostle Paul wrote to those who followed Jesus. Paul wrote from prison. He told them about his life. Sometimes he had plenty. At other times, he had very little. Sometimes Paul had food; at other times it was hunger that he possessed. In response, Paul wrote that he was learning something about God and joy as he surrendered to these varying seasons. "I know how to be brought low, and I know how to abound," he said. "In any and every circumstance, I have learned the secret of facing plenty and hunger, abundance and need. I can do all things through him who strengthens me" (Phil. 4:12–13).

Our own testimony is meant to follow Paul's into this same direction. We too will learn to say that we know how to be brought low and how to abound. We are learning that whatever time it is, Jesus is there with us. The

Preacher foreshadows Paul's point. No matter what time it is, we learn to adjust to it on the basis of the hope and purpose that God is in it, that everything has a beauty to it by which the Preacher declares that every disquieting and delightful moment under the sun has been fitted by God for his purposes. With God, everything fits, nothing is wasted or lost.[4] God does not abandon one second of a life under the sun. No disquiet is God forsaken. No true delight is God neglected. Joseph pointed us to this beauty, these purpose-drenched seconds, when he looked at all the pain, the reoccurring tears and the long years of wreckage that his brothers had perpetrated, and he interpreted it all by saying, "You meant evil against me, but God meant it for good" (Gen. 50:20). Paul takes up Joseph's message. He sees it from the vantage point of Jesus. He preaches it to the people of God. There is nothing in all creation, no moment under the sun, that "will be able to separate us from the love of God in Christ Jesus our Lord" (Rom. 8:38–39).

Fourth, just as a farm can sit on a field with rocks thrown into it, so our lots are given within a generation under the sun. It might be that we were born into a time to kill or a time to heal, a time of love or a time of hate, a time for war or a time for peace. When the Preacher speaks about killing, hatred, or war, we remind ourselves that the whole poem is "not prescriptive, but rather descriptive."[5] He is not telling us what we must choose. Rather, he is describing the choices people make and the circumstances we find ourselves in. Again, "the poet is describing what occurs under the sun; he is not making moral pronouncements."[6]

Ruth and Naomi lost their husbands, endured famine, and tried to build a new life during the age of the Judges—a generation in which everyone did what was right in their own eyes. So we too may find ourselves in times of war or killing that we would not have chosen, facing circumstances that we wish were not ours to face. Or we may find ourselves gratefully born into a generation of peace and healing. My life has been surrounded by war. If I were born a few years earlier or later I could have known the life of a soldier. Born in a year that I did not choose, I watched those older and younger than I go to war.

Finally, our response to our lot amid these varying seasons isn't robotic or staged. God intended that in our lots we would experience a full range of emotional expression. For those who refuse to cry, surrender to God is something that must wisely be learned, for there is a time to weep. Sometimes under the sun, tears are the only appropriate and God-given response that a human being can muster. For those who resist laughter, apprenticeship with God will knock the crust off of your closed heart and disciple you into cheek muscles that pull upward and eyebrows that rise. Laughter and weeping are gifts of God for the seasons that ramble through our lots. There is a time, as David illustrates for us, to dance before the Lord in our lives. Celebration is a gift from God for our lots in these vain days of our short lives. The fussbudget who forever shushes bodily movement in thanksgiving has something of wisdom yet to learn from God.

SPECULATIONS DO NOT HELP US

Perhaps the reason the Preacher recalls us to our lot is because when we look out at these disquiets and delights that rumble through our lives under the sun, we are prone to spend time in speculating about things that we cannot answer. The Preacher gives us an example.

> Who knows whether the spirit of man goes upward
> and the spirit of the beast goes down into the earth?
> (Eccl. 3:21)

Some in his day suggested that animals don't go to heaven as humans do after they die. Others said differently. The Preacher's point isn't that he doubts the afterlife. As

135

we will see below, he clearly believes in one (Eccl. 3:17). His point is that we just don't know the answer to such questions. Because there is a great deal that we cannot know, we ought instead to seek what is truly good, not in endless speculating but in tending to the God-given callings and joys of our lot.

> So I saw that there is nothing better than that a man should rejoice in his work, for that is his lot. Who can bring him to see what will be after him? (Eccl. 3:22)

In any given season, we are tempted to imagine, think, speculate, meditate on, worry about, and mull over everything that we do not know about the times in which we find ourselves. The Preacher says that the way forward in our seasons is not found in rehearsing what we do not know, but in remaining faithful to what we do.

A parable surrounding St. Anthony seeks to capture this point. Anthony felt restless in his place. Struck with boredom, melancholy, and a wandering mind, he asked God how to be rescued from his troubled thoughts. No immediate answer came. Later, Anthony "saw a man like himself sitting down and working, then standing up to pray; then sitting down again to make a plait of palm leaves, then standing up again to pray." Viewing this, Anthony heard an angel of the Lord "saying to him, 'Do this and you will be cured.'" Anthony saw in this that his way out of what troubled his mind was found in staying his course and attending to what he knew to do in front of him—prayer and his work, prayer and his work. In this way, a road through the unknowns and inward trials of the season was found.[7]

The Preacher expands upon this theme in Ecclesiastes 8 and 11.

In Ecclesiastes 8, the Preacher uses an illustration with a king and his servants. In the presence of the king and the king's use of power, "the wise heart will know the proper time and the just way" to think and to act (Eccl. 8:5).

Learning this wisdom for doing what needs doing when the time warrants it is necessary, not only with kings, but in life. "There is a time and a way for everything," the Preacher declares, "although man's trouble lies heavy on him" (Eccl. 8:6).

And though we sadly have the power to hurt each other under the sun (Eccl. 8:9), the Preacher reminds us that "no man has power to retain the spirit, or power over the day of death." Neither can we stop war or the damage done by neighbors who try to make life work by means of wickedness (Eccl. 8:8). We cannot stop the fact that hypocrisy continues and those who indulge it are often honored (Eccl. 8:10), while humble men and women of integrity and charity are often overlooked and mistreated (Eccl. 8:14).

Therefore, within this vain context under the sun, to spend our season in speculation is fruitless for a person. "For he does not know what is to be, for who can tell him how it will be?" (Eccl. 8:7). When sportscasters analyze, pontificate, and forecast a sports event, for all of their talk, no one actually knows who will win until the game is played. So it is with us in our lives.

In our seasons and times, we are like those who watch a movie. The person next to us wants us to talk during it. "Why is she doing that?" "Oh, no, what's going to happen?" "Where is he going?" Our response remains, "I don't know, we have to wait and watch the movie in order to find out." Often, the only way to find out what is happening in life is to watch quietly and wait.

So it is with how this under-the-sun speech constantly asks us to generate energy, chatter, and jibber jabber in our seasons about things which no one can actually know.

> Then I saw all the work of God, that man cannot find out the work that is done under the sun. However much man may toil in seeking, he will not find it out. Even though a wise man claims to know, he cannot find it out. (Eccl. 8:17)

137

What then are we to do? Two things.

First, he repeats his conviction that we turn from misguided uses of power and empty speculation and instead give ourselves to God's provision of joy found within our ordinary lot (Eccl. 8:15). Second, as we will explore below, we are to take heart in the ultimate purpose, nearness, and judgment of God.

> Though a sinner does evil a hundred times and prolongs his life, yet I know that it will be well with those who fear God, because they fear before him. But it will not be well with the wicked . . . because he does not fear before God. (Eccl. 8:12–13)

In Ecclesiastes 11, the Preacher uses the analogy of a farmer to reinforce this ordinary rhythmic way in which we are to navigate our seasons. Our speculations cannot solve certain mysteries. "You do not know the way the spirit comes to the bones in the womb of a woman with child, so you do not know the work of God who makes everything" (Eccl. 11:5).

Since we are tempted to get stuck trying to solve what we cannot know, the Preacher gives us an illustration of a farmer who resists his work because storm clouds rise. Speculating about the clouds, the farmer will neither sow nor reap. He will have no produce.

"But," he might say, "it looked like it was going to rain! The wind was starting to blow!" "The trees might fall!" Such a farmer forgets that he does not know "what disaster may happen on earth," whether the threatening storm will amount to anything or simply fade with a fuss (Eccl. 11:1–4). Storms come, winds blow, trees fall. Who knows whether it will happen now or ever? This is beyond what we can control. All that we can do is to give ourselves to tend what we've been given.

If we can neither control nor predict what will happen when the season to sow or harvest comes, what is a farmer to do? He needs to go ahead and cast his bread upon the waters, to attend to what he has and to make use of it (Eccl. 11:1). Like Miriam putting the baby Moses in a basket on the waters, we do not know whether prosperity or ruin will come. So, the Middle Eastern farmer sows his seed on the flood plain[8] or sends boats that will take produce to invest.[9] We give our portions to this and to that opportunity within our work that presents itself (Eccl. 11:2). Instead of rehearsing imaginary dooms or fortunes or spinning his wheels in idle speculations, he rather needs to attend to what is in front of him in the lot God has given him with the daily rhythm that morning and evening provides. Why? Because who but God knows how it will all turn out?

> In the morning sow your seed, and at evening withhold not your hand, for you do not know which will prosper, this or that, or whether both alike will be good. Light is sweet, and it is pleasant for the eyes to see the sun. (Eccl. 11:6–7)

When the unknown taunts your mind within the season you find yourself, give yourself to the next thing in the place you are. Knit your palms into rope. Then stand for a while and pray. Knit. Pray. Knit. Pray. Eat. Drink. Enjoy your family. And notice the sun. Give thanks for its light. Take pleasure in its gift. God is near. This small way and tiny rhythm resemble the grand way of life for which human beings were given Eden. Our way forward more often than not is found where we are.

When a disquieting thing breaks someone's life, what do we do? We bring food. We wash dishes for them. We sit, listen in the quiet, and offer our space-giving presence. We take a walk. We send a card. We spend a few days at a friend's home. A child offers his Batman stickers or her drawing. We do the next thing at work. We wait, watch, and attend to morning and evening, in order to find how it will all turn out. Similarly, when a delightful thing blesses someone's life, the things we do are the same, but with laughter. We bring food, drink, gifts, cards, stickers, and ourselves.

In our lot, the misuse of power and speculation tempts us all around to turn to such strivings as a means of controlling the madness we see and feel under the sun. The apostle Peter heard speculation about his friend, the apostle John. Everyone was gossiping about it and trying to figure it out. Peter asked Jesus to enter the speculation and to answer Peter's desire to know about it. Jesus responded by letting Peter know that John's future was in Jesus' hands. "What is that to you?" Jesus then asked. "You follow me!" (John 21:22).

JESUS AND THE SEASONS

Jesus was born and this into a time for war. Rome occupied and ruled his people and land. Zealots plotted. Rebels skirmished. Soldiers roamed the landscape on the streets, at the stores, near places of business. Herod put to death every two-year-old boy in the region. Death came. That would have been in the lore of his community; it would have been talked about year after year. It would have been part of the history he learned in school. Jesus and his family fled as refugees in the night to Egypt. What they had gathered had to be cast away. A time came when they could return and build again.

There were times when Jesus was silent and those who should have stood up in his defense said nothing. He was building a kingdom which some sought to tear down. He was seeking to tear down kingdoms that demons and illusions sought to build.

There was a time when his disciples heard him speak and felt his embrace. The garden came. Betrayal rose. Silence and distance closed the doors.

Jesus saw people losing, seeking toy treasures, and turning away, like that rich young man who came to him.

And Jesus loved him, but the man turned away from Jesus and walked away sad. Jesus saw people weeping. There was a time to mourn, in their diseases, in their pains, in their aging, in their ordinary life stages. Jesus too wept.

There was a time to dance and to laugh. Jesus knew what it was to see people dancing inappropriately the way the prodigal son likely did. He knew what it was to be around prostitutes and sinners. He would have known the kind of parties that they had and seen that kind of dancing.

But Jesus also knew what it was to dance at a celebration, a Jewish celebration, when the whole community would hold hands and they would have danced together, in worship, together welcoming the lost son home.

When disease shrank back at his words, and legs, minds, skin, and eyes were freed again to do what they were built to do, do you think Jesus stood there stoically when someone was healed right before their eyes? If their legs could move again, they would have danced. Right then and there, they would have danced. He too would have laughed with joy.

I'm sure Jesus had to tear down tables, a woodpile, a scrap pile. He knew how to build with wood. He knew what it was to see killing. He knew what it was to plant, to pluck up. And Jesus knows what it means to die.

Jesus experienced our seasons and times. His sympathy with us abounds. If you're a stepparent needing help, or you are a new parent, or you think you might become one, or you're pregnant, then you're reading books, you're talking to people. You want to know what it's like. If you start a new job, you talk to people who know what it's like to start that new job because you're trying to find people who can resonate with you. If you have some type of addiction, if you've been through some type of trauma, if you've had some type of celebration, you want people to resonate with you. We long for empathy and it's often in short supply. And the whole picture given in the Bible is that God has entered life under the sun and in Jesus taken it all.

So when you're sitting sad on your chair, in your living room, the message for you is that Jesus knew the times. He too cried as you cry. He too has been abandoned, the way some of you have been abandoned. He too has overcome the way many of you have overcome. He too has sung with poetry, in the brokenness of betrayal like some of you. He too has died, as we all will. But in him, the sting of death has died.

Eden would describe only one side of the Preacher's poem. Eden was a place of birth, a place of planting, of healing, a place of building up, a place of laughter, a place of dancing, a place of embracing, of seeking, of keeping, of sowing. Heaven foreshadowed!

But under the sun, we foretaste the absence of God. Hellish foreshadowings tend the presence of death, of plucking up, of killing, of breaking down, of weeping, of mourning, of casting away, of losing, of tearing, of silence, of war. Jesus entered once-Eden to recover what was lost, to foreshadow what comes, the heavenly kingdom that waits.

QUESTIONS FOR DISCUSSIONS

1. How are lawnmowers like people and what does this have to do with the teaching in this section of Ecclesiastes?

2. Talk about the grace and wisdom of being prepared ahead of time for what comes. How do the Preacher and ultimately Jesus do this for us?

3. What is a disquiet? What is a delight? Which kind of season are you more prone to try to avoid in your life?

4. How does the Preacher teach us to see time? How can this help us as we relate with our neighbors? How does time point us to Jesus?

5. In contrast to Job's friends with Job, why does it matter that we make adjustments according to the season that we or our neighbors find ourselves in?

6. How do the apostle Paul's words in 2 Corinthians 6:10 summarize this section of Ecclesiastes? What grace does this summary offer to you?

7. Why are speculations fruitless? Why then do we want to engage with them?

8. What do the seasons show us about Jesus?

CHAPTER EIGHT

CHURCH, UNDER THE SUN

"It pleases me to stand in silence here."[1]

W hen I was a kid, we sang a little song as we acted it out with our hands. "This is the church," we'd sing as we made the palms of our hands touch each other and lengthened our fingers into lining up and facing their undersides. "This is the steeple," we'd continue as we collapsed all of our finger length into resting except for our two index fingers, which we left pointing together up into the air. Then we'd sing, "open the doors and there are the people," as we opened our thumbs like doors and then turned our hands upside down and inside out, which revealed all of our fingers interconnected and moving about like a congregation.

That old song points to something true when we use the word *church*. The "church" consists of the people. The people are the church regardless of buildings. But the church often meets in a church. Buildings with steeples or walls dot the landscape. Houses of God are everywhere in the world. The house of God and what we do when we open its doors and walk through into its sanctuary forms the Preacher's topic as he begins Ecclesiastes 5. By his doing so, we learn that talking about a "house of God" with each other and our neighbors makes sense if we are to account for what we experience in this life under the sun. Dealing with houses of God forms part of our common human story.

CHURCH AS AN ATHEIST MAKER

In that light, not all of our experiences are pleasant. For example, Czeslaw Milosz, the poet, once wrote to Thomas Merton, the monk, that he at one time resisted allowing his sons to attend church because he "did not want to make atheists out of them."[2] It sounds strange at first, the idea that sometimes acquaintance with church can repel one's faith, especially to those who give thanks for church. It has often been in church among church folks that God has recovered my sense of him. Cups of soup and Tupperware tubs of casserole have accompanied the hugs, the prayers, and the hope-spoken tears of those who have both celebrated and cried with me to God in such houses. Sunday morning meetings in those houses have provided me with gifts of truth, repentance, solid ground, forgiveness, grace, and relational wisdom. Bible words spoken in Jesus with human teeth and tongue have come to me at times as if God himself stood before me, spoke them to me, and by them lifted my head. In short, the house and the people of God have been God's means to keep me sane in him amid the madness of my own heart and the strivings after wind that hollow us out.

That being said, God houses have also rabble-roused me, and this gives me great empathy for Milosz's sentiment. I too have been tempted to quit them. At times, I have asked them for bread and instead they have put an agitated snake in my bag. Their death bites and venom teeth have paralyzed my joints and muscles. Many nights, they've flopped me over like a fish and filleted me down the middle. My innards have come out only to get quickly discarded into the trash.

Jesus affirms the sentiment. He spoke of those who by means of their church work created adherents who

146

were children "of hell" (Matt. 23:15). Such congregants at church are like those who try to help us in our fog by flashing on the bright lights, never recognizing that high beams impair rather than aid the sight of those who must travel through haze and mist. Bright light and fog blur and blend, merge and reflect back in such a way that we must squint and blink while the road ahead whites out and grows scarily hidden from view. Even genuine disciples can act like bright-lighting and hellish children, repellent to those in the fog—and all of this in the name of God. Peter, the apostle, found this out (Mark 8:33). So have I. The idea of "church" therefore triggers a trauma response in some. Under the sun, "church" and "God" can flatten negatively into synonyms. Such neighbors want no part of either.

In some places under the sun, our human neighbors know nothing of church at all. Church buildings sit abandoned in neighborhoods like a heart shape that two young lovers once carved into a tree. They cut their laughter into the wood, only later to regret their pledge. One of them went back at night to scrape off the names. These years later, their bark carvings remain but few see them. When someone does venture to see them, the names are unpronounceable and the love is gone. Philip Larkin captured some of this in his poem "Church Going." "When churches shall fall completely out of use . . . Shall we regard them as unlucky places?"[3]

So, when Solomon begins Ecclesiastes 5 with the words "when you go to the house of God," did he understand the risk of neighbor conversation to which he called us? I think he did. He spoke of church, not naively, but as it exists actually under the sun. By doing so, he teaches us to do the same. When you go to the house of God, he said, "guard your steps" (Eccl. 5:1). Church under the sun warrants caution. Even church that worships God as the Bible reveals him. The wise therefore have this in common with those who point out the chipped paint and rotten wood of church.

WHEAT AND WEEDS

Why? What is it about church that requires our caution?

First, we must guard our steps because fools run amok in church. Look at these verses. Notice how the Preacher contrasts foolish churchgoing with what is wise (Eccl. 5:1, 3–4). By pointing out the contrast, the Preacher teaches us that church people are often a motley crew. The banter between wisdom and folly that saturates the marketplace (Prov. 9) does not retreat as if a moat or a force field stood between it and the church building. Jesus put this fact into parable. Weeds and wheat grow together in God's fields until the harvest comes (Matt. 13:24–30).

Many neighbors struggle with this idea. Churchgoing neighbors are tempted to believe that no weeds are welcome in a house of God. They are forever reforming, weeding out, and narrowing down the membership list. They speak to our neighbors about church only if they think they are worthy of getting in. Such neighbors are surprised to find sinners in church. The Preacher doesn't view church under the sun in this way.

For other neighbors, if someone claims to follow God, goes to church, and then says or does things that malign God's name or hurts their neighbors, they are prone in their pain to leave off, not only with church, but also with God. Such neighbors are surprised to find sin in churches. The Preacher possesses no such surprise.

What remains challenging under the sun is that we are made for community (Eccl. 4:9–12). If we do not go to church, we will try to find connection with people some other way: Podcasts, chat rooms, local organizations and groups. As we seek community, most of us come to the painful awareness that fools and folly exist in every gathering under the sun. What we try to escape from church people we encounter among nonchurch people. Sometimes the greatest fights aren't in church but on a Little League field or in a school board gathering or political rally or even in our own family reunions. Whether in a church or out of it, people under the sun exhibit folly.

In pain and protest, some neighbors isolate themselves altogether. The loneliness haunts us, though. We converse with our thoughts only and always. Left to ourselves, we have only ourselves. It isn't long before we learn that we can hurt ourselves—the folly within us leads us astray and lets us down. We can quarrel even with ourselves.

So, the tension emerges. We are made for community and worship, and we function best within this arrangement (as Adam and Eve did). But, this side of Eden, folly infests the houses we need. Honest about all of this, the Preacher still believes that we needn't abandon the house of God. Instead, knowing what is in there, we step inside and seek mending for the walls, while those same walls shelter us for the night.

Consequently, instead of haranguing neighbors to get to church or belittling their pain and whitewashing bad church experiences, wisdom beckons us to honesty, empathy, and human truth telling. "Yes," we say with a sigh, "the church can wound."

We go further and admit, "Sometimes the grandest fools are those wearing Sunday clothes and carrying Bibles. Sometimes I have been one," we confess.

Then with common human honesty and empathy we affirm, "It makes sense that you would feel skittish at the thought of church."

Then we gently testify to the grace that we ourselves have needed as it relates to church. "I've appreciated a wise man in the Bible who cautioned us to watch our steps when we go to church," we offer. "Somehow in his caution he still attended," we say. "I'm trying too to learn what he meant," we conclude.

Then we give an invitation, not only to church, but to doing life together under the sun. "If you ever want to enter this caution and learning with me, I'd welcome it."

With that invitation we wait and pray and by grace we love our neighbor.

A CLOSER LOOK AT THE WEEDS

The Preacher not only recognizes the mixture of wheat and weeds that coexist in churches under the sun, he goes further to actually name the kinds of misuse that church people will perpetrate. In his memoir *Losing My Religion*,[4] William Lobdell recounts how, as a reporter on the church scene in America for a well-known newspaper, he could no longer believe in God. What tore at his soul the most was the willingness of congregants in churches across America to hurt others or to defend the ones who do. His memoir is grateful in tone and earnest. He sets out to name plainly the misuse of things done regularly in God's name. The Preacher and William have a common purpose. They both plainly name foolery done in God's name. But as we will see, the Preacher arrives nonetheless at a very different conclusion.

To begin, foolish churchgoers express a clueless or blind hypocrisy. They do evil but do not know it (Eccl. 5:1). In saying this, the Preacher clearly states that people will do terrible things while wearing the garb of God. More painful and infuriating is the fact that many will do so blindly. They will do violence to neighbors and actually think that God loves it that way (John 16:2). Jesus illustrated this fact by referring to "blind guides." "If the blind lead the blind, both will fall into a pit" (Matt. 15:14). Sometimes under the sun, it is religious folks who are the ones who smother us in the mud.

But even blind guides with violent hands can recover in Jesus. Even those who do not know what they are doing can hear the words of the Savior, "Forgive them, for they know not what they do." Even a blind guide like Saul of Tarsus doing harm in the name of God can be saved.

150

Ironically, foolish churchgoers recognize a need for sacrifice. But they look to themselves and to external appearances. "The sacrifice of fools" (Eccl. 5:1) indicates those who take part in religious ceremony and observances and who look to that participation in order to justify themselves as being close to God and good among people. But it isn't sacrifice but mercy that God calls us to (Ps. 51:16–17). Woefully unaware of their true selves, they put people off by their way of relating to people and doing business. Persona becomes a way of life for them. They think that dislike for them is due to the fact that they are persecuted for righteousness' sake, when in fact their arrogant behavior warrants the rancor.

Jesus put this truth into a parable. Two men went into God's house to pray, the one a mouthy Bible man, the other a known sinner. While the Bible man puts his good deeds into prose, the sinner beats his breast from shame and cries from his heart to God. The moral of Jesus' story? It is the sinner and not the righteous man whom God justifies (Luke 18:9–14). We are not meant to use church as a cloak to cover our ugly ways or as a talisman to wish them away. Church is meant to disrupt our denial. We are meant to learn, there in God's house, how to unvarnish our lives before him. The Preacher apprentices us who follow God to resist putting makeup on the church. Instead, we plainly name for and with our neighbors the ignorant and arrogant actions that church people often do.

This does not mean that we agree with some neighbors who suggest therefore that the world would be better off if religion died. While church people can do harmful things, the Preacher locates the problem not with church, but with the soul of every human being. Human beings seek out "many schemes" (Eccl. 7:29). Most of the crime in my city, and there is a great deal of it, has nothing to do with God. Most bullies on playgrounds aren't pushing smaller kids because of their belief in God. Many nations of violence have harmed peoples for reasons that have

151

nothing to do with worship. The wise admit with Solomon that the bent heart of a human being can wield a baseball bat, a bank transaction, or even a prayer to harm another human being. Whatever tool remains near at hand the seething heart will take up.

The Preacher names something further for us too. Foolery loves religious talk. Fools possess a religion of the unstoppable mouth. Foolish churchgoers have little tolerance for quiet. They always chatter. The Preacher describes "a fool's voice with many words" (Eccl. 5:3). These clueless performers constantly multiply god-talk, as if God is impressed with what they say, and as if their salvation resides in their ability to vacuum up every floor just by pushing their speech back and forth over it.

Furthermore, foolish churchgoers assume that what they think and feel is synonymous with what God thinks and feels. If they think it, they must say it. If they feel it, they must relieve it by means of orality. Dreams, those day and night imaginings and goals, are always from God and never indicative of something potentially illusory within them. They are first-draft people, living daily on unmeditated speech. Patience is a nuisance. Taking time to think is a waste of time. Plans must be made. Visions enacted. Great things must be quickly done. For them, haste, constant talk, and busying oneself identify the hallmarks of those who should be in church (Eccl. 5:2–3).

But for the Preacher, "when dreams increase and words grow many, there is vanity" (Eccl. 5:7). Quantity of church talk and activity does not indicate the presence or blessing of God. Jesus will take up Solomon's theme and fulfill it. "And when you pray," Jesus says, "do not heap up empty phrases as the Gentiles do, for they think that they will be heard for their many words" (Matt. 6:7). In fact, when Jesus teaches us to pray, he gives us only a handful of words that take less than a minute to read (Matt. 6:9–13).

The fool gets antsy and disagrees. God hears us if we talk a lot. So, we excuse, spin, explain, divert, pontificate, and pronounce, and claim our words are his. Quantity of dreams and words, constant increase in plans and strategies, this is where our strengths lie. "Look at all we've done and said" becomes the measure of godliness. Bigger equals better. More equals God's blessing. But the fool in church does not know that his words about God are spoken in vain. He does not know that to take God's name in vain has little to do with four-letter words and more to do with professing to follow God while our lives show that we know nothing truly of his character.

In addition, foolish churchgoers hastily make promises and pledges. They make excuses for not keeping their promises. The big speech gave them applause for the moment. Once the applause is gone, they have little motivation for following through when the crowd dies down. Church becomes a means for self-advancement and promotion. Emotional bursts and hasty reasoning signify the car of choice. Business practices are sloppy but the hype astounds. They always have a religious reason for why they cannot do what they pledged to do. They love poorly and tell you how it was God who justifies what they did or didn't do. The foolish churchgoer's word is not his bond (Eccl. 5:4–6).

So, the Preacher tells us to guard our steps when it comes to church because sometimes when we walk into the sanctuary what we find there is evil, bombast, arrogance, and slick speech with poor relational follow-through.

Solomon does two things by telling this to us. One, he lets his hearers know that he is not naive toward what goes on in a church. Neither then must we be. Church under the sun isn't heaven. Second, he lets his hearers know that the presence of foolish people using God's name does not imply the absence of a genuine work of God. Yes, some church folks are spiritually deaf, disdaining of patience, unacquainted with waiting, and arrogant regarding the importance they ascribe to their own thoughts, feelings, imaginations, and excuses. Self-absorbed, they are clueless regarding the evil they inflict on their neighbors. In fact, without the grace of Jesus, none of us would be rescued from such foolery. But instead of quitting the house of God, the Preacher has something else in mind.

A CLOSER LOOK AT THE WHEAT

In his memoir, *Blue Like Jazz*,[5] Donald Miller recounts how a few Christians attempted to engage an annual campus-wide party. As people ran about drunk, stoned, and naked, Donald and his friends decided to set up a confession booth in their midst. The catch was this. If a neighbor should choose to enter the booth, it was Donald who would take the lead and confess his sins as a Christian. The Christian would become the confessor and the "heathen" neighbor would hear it.

The time for the party arrived. Donald and his friends were nervous. Would anyone come into the booth? In a moving narrative, Donald describes how one by one people came. These neighbors reeked of party leftovers, but many were also shocked, moved, tear-soaked, and humbled as Donald confessed his own regret regarding how, as a follower of Jesus, he and others treated some of them and the campus. He wanted them to know that he followed Jesus but that Jesus was different from him, that Jesus would not sin against them the way his followers are prone to, and that he is altogether beautiful in his grace to save us from ourselves. Instead of quitting those campus neighbors or yelling at them in protest, Donald and his friends risked engaging them by means of trying to embody something true about Jesus by their way of doing life among them.

Donald and his friends attempted in their flawed way to approach a concept that the Preacher seems to have in mind. Rather than quitting the church or yelling at it, we instead cultivate a way of life that recovers what the house of God was meant to be.

This recovery begins with a routine regarding the house of God. The Preacher uses the word *when*. "*When* you go to the house of God," he says (Eccl. 5:1). *If* means maybe. *When* designates something certain. A routine gives a chance to try at something over and again. In doing the same thing regularly, we have the opportunity to let the thing that we are revisiting shape us. Like an athlete or artist or craftsman, we become familiar, expert, or veteran in something by virtue of long and repeated experience with it. A swimmer doesn't get something and struggles for several practices. Some practices are boring; others are spectacular. The assumption isn't that the swimmer should quit. The assumption is that the swimmer needs more time, more practice, more opportunities to come at it and to learn. So it is with the house of God.

Cultivating a weekly or daily rhythm or routine is commonplace. In fact, some things in life we cherish to the point that those who know us will say, "*When* are you going to do such and so again?" rather than "if you do that again" or "I'm surprised you are trying that again." Sometimes these assumed routines rise out of necessity. We set an alarm clock to repeat a rhythm of work or exercise each day in order to provide for our livelihood or the well-being of an animal, a tool, or a plot of ground. At other times, we meet weekly for leisure to play cards, to enjoy sport, or to walk in the garden or practice an instrument. We watch a favorite television show each week or get tickets to secure a season of seats. We pen in our schedules and guard them in order to meet regularly with a family member or good friend. Even our addictions lead us to secure a routine of making sure that other things take a "back seat." We identify a place and time to exercise or to write or to mow our lawns or to read to our kids, brush their teeth, and get them ready for bed. The pattern establishes a way of life—a way that we use time to keep coming back to something that matters. The Preacher isn't asking us therefore to do something unique. Rather, he is asking us to take the same routine making that we use for other things under the sun, and to apply this to the house of God. The house of God isn't meant for one-time experiences or for an every-time-a-spectacular-time-or-we-quit kind of approach. "When" indicates a certainty regarding something that we want to come back to again and again. "When" indicates our pursuit of apprenticeship, a way of life.

Then the Preacher indicates that as we cultivate this ongoing acquaintance with the house of God, we are meant to pursue and learn a particular quality of being from the experience. In other words, we must counter the foolery of churchgoing, but not by quitting or fighting. We counterpoint folly by going to church wisely. The means by which we overcome evil is by embodying what is good and establishing in our life and community an alternate vision and way of approaching church. What is this alternate way?

To begin, we go to church in order to learn how to slow our tongues and to quiet our hearts. We are meant by means of churchgoing to unlearn our hasty hearts and to detox our rash voices (Eccl. 5:1). Instead of asserting ourselves, and filling the space with what we propose it needs, we encounter a space that is already purposed by a being who has already asserted himself. Our task is to receive and surrender to the will of another. Wise churchgoing apprentices us in humility. It teaches us to listen. According to the Preacher, churchgoers become humble listeners who possess a stamina for waiting, a capacity for patience, an esteem for the time that true reflection requires.

To clarify at this point, the Preacher is not talking about music. He isn't saying that we sing somber songs, and that no one can move or make a sound. Listening doesn't require stiffness, lethargy, or funeral dirges. Likewise, being quiet, glaring at kids who aren't, and shushing the shuffling of pant legs or the strumming of a guitar do not mean that anyone is listening to God or cultivating humility in his presence. The Preacher isn't attacking joyful music and instruments. He is attacking haste, verbosity, impatience, and arrogance. Sometimes church folks pick on the piano player for playing too loudly, all the while they seem oblivious to the fact that what God is trying to teach in church is his patience and humility. A loud drummer can be a humble man. A quiet singer can be a hasty and rash human being.

Why do we draw near to resist our personal haste of thought, feeling, and word? Because church is the house *of God.* God presents himself for our contemplation and adoration. Whatever we utter in church, we do so in his very presence. Moreover, God is God and we are not. We "utter a word before God, for God is in heaven and you are on earth" (Eccl. 5:2). Churchgoing is a God-hallowing activity. When we go, we keep trying again to hear him teach us to listen and to reorient our lives under the sun around his voice rather than ours, his character rather than ours, his grace rather than our performance, his ways rather than that which ransacks us under the sun. When God is present, people become quieter—not out of fear of being abused but out of a recognition that true good, power, beauty, and wisdom have entered the room. "God is the one you must fear" (Eccl. 5:7). Most of us, though, naturally fear losing our dreams or approvals or vow opportunities.

But, if God was sitting at the table and a question was asked, he would be the first one whom everyone looked to for an answer (if they were humble). So it is when we enter his house. We are not made quiet because God has a temper and we don't want to set him off. His anger and ability to destroy our works (Eccl. 5:6) do not describe the bully who uses anger to control us or the violent-tempered person who needs anger management and with whom we walk on "egg shells." Rather, he gets angry at what we would hope he would. He does not intend to approve or favor those who use his name and his house in order to do evil to others. Those who harm neighbors in his name, who justify it with their blindness, and who use church to exalt their own words, dreams, and plans are opposed by

God. In other words, God opposes the proud. He disrupts the hypocrite. Those who misuse church in order to promote folly under the sun bother God.

For those of us who have been victimized by church folks, what the Preacher tells us here is great news! His anger at the evil done in church by fools both vindicates and upholds the sanity of those who have been misused. The works he destroys are the religious works of foolish churchgoers. God does what we long for. He will judge the churchgoing hypocrite.

On the other hand, for those of us who go to church foolishly, the Preacher is warning us. We cannot fool God by our religiosity. Jesus takes up this theme. He begins to shout with anger and lament, not at the woman at the well, or the tax collector or the sinner. Instead, he hurls prophetic woes with relentless force upon those who have been using church as a means of selfishly advancing themselves, arrogantly harming others, and blindly distorting the character and work of God (Matt. 23).

Consequently, we learn in his presence not to act on our impulsive thought or our ugly emotion. Human dreams and vows, so urgent in the moment, need not feel ultimate or lasting. What God dreams and what God has vowed increasingly enthrall us. Excuses fade because we are less tempted to use church in order to advance ourselves. We don't have to manipulate those who reside with church, like priests or attendants or "messengers," because we are less inclined to use church as a means of trying to prove something to God or to keep up appearances. We are already known. Our evils are already found out. Our denials are less and less interesting. Clean and humble truth about God and about us is taking center stage. We are made quiet in the presence of a vibrant storyteller, an intimate lover, a merciful knower of our worst moments. The absence of haste rests us. Freed from having to spin words, contentment finds us. God is here. Finally, sanity and grace find us. We can rest now. We are learning to embody an alternative way of churchgoing. This alternative way has little to do with musical style, vision statements, and fonts. It has more to do with a quality of being that God intends by routine to cultivate in his people. As this happens, folly has a rival, grace and wisdom grow, the house of God gets rehabbed under the sun until he comes.

GOD AND HIS HOUSE

In Solomon's day, the house of God was a temple that stood like a deeply rooted tree offering shade amid the delights and disquiets that blustered through the place and its peoples. This standing temple was to remind everyone that God didn't quit when Eden died. Eden, you remember, had no church building, no hellish congregants spouting off. Eden itself was all pulpit and pew. Every bit of it formed a sanctuary in which Adam and Eve could give themselves to the glory and enjoyment of the God who loved them and for whom they lived. Eden was a God-hallowed place. Each leaf and parcel of dirt, each bit of rock or bark, along with every creature bone and wing, scale and shell, fur and skin, existed as if adorned with the delight of God's merriment. The countenance of everything radiated the joy of its having received God's hearty benediction. Good tidings of God bounded forth and belly-laughed. No hidden corner suffered rot. Eden was what church is meant to be, a place in which God draws close to let us know him. Knowing him, we are whole and home.

Ideally, our church structures, whether they are made of bricks or stones or sticks; whether they are put together in abandoned buses, secret basements, or rock shells or on the barren sands; these are meant to pronounce that God has left neither us nor this wreckage under the sun. Instead, God has come to dwell beneath this sun. He inhabits the heat with us. Though he needn't do so, he makes his dwelling here where we live. The house of God, flawed as it sometimes is because of human misuse in his name, still symbolizes the presence of God with us. That God has kept a house in our neighborhood makes its compelling case for our attendance amid the vandalisms of our under-the-sun graffiti.

So, Solomon makes clear (and so must we) that God and his house are not equal. Our personal experiences with vipers placed into our spiritual bags colored with Bible verses tell us as much. But Solomon teaches us the point plainly. When he built and dedicated the house for God that his dad, King David, envisioned, Solomon knew that God didn't limit himself to its man-made walls. It was important for everyone to understand this too, lest they mistake the house for God himself. In front of everyone Solomon prayed:

> But will God indeed dwell on the earth? Behold, heaven and the highest heaven cannot contain you; how much less this house that I have built! (1 Kings. 8:27)

Solomon assures us regarding what Jesus later taught us to pray, "Our Father [is] in heaven" (Matt. 6:9). But not even heaven, much less the walls made by human hands, can encompass God's dwelling place (1 Kings 8:30, 34, 36, 39).

This distinction between God and his house makes enough sense. Any of us who own a house, rent an apartment, or build a hut within which to live knows full well that we are not our dwelling places. Yet, when we are old or some unexpected turn in life takes our house from us, we are prone to forget. We can act as if our lives will go the way the house goes. To lose the house is to lose ourselves. We are prone to this with God's house too. We are tempted to believe that foreclosure on the house indicates a bankruptcy of God's ways and will. So, in time, the apostle Paul followed Jesus and paralleled Solomon in his preaching about God to his Bibleless neighbors. "The God who made the world and everything in it," Paul declared, "being Lord of heaven and earth, does not live in temples made by man" (Acts 17:24).

Knock the walls down and God remains. Crumble our plaques and rip up our pictures, but God's character goes on. Sell our building and send our congregants elsewhere, but God's accounts remain full and his doors open. The house of God, then, is like a green branch pushing its way out of a blackened tree stump; an unyielding flower that still blooms amid the grey ash of a bombed-out village; a persecuted man forced to work knee-deep in human dung, who sings praises still to Jesus. The house of God reminds us that God has not abandoned the raging world to a life without witness to himself. But though it witnesses to him, it does not exhaust, limit, or consume him. Church buildings are not genie bottles. The genie stays trapped inside the bottle unless we let him out, and afterward he is put back in. A phone in a phone booth has no life beyond the windowed boundaries. We leave the phone booth, and the phone does not go with us. But this is not so when we leave God's house. God has a life outside his house, a connection beyond the booth.

THE PURPOSE OF GOD'S HOUSE

So, Solomon dedicated God's house with prayer. The Preacher was also a pray-er. His prayer reveals to us the nature of God's presence under the sun.

Solomon's prayer teaches us that God's house is hospitable. In fact, anyone can come there to pray, to seek forgiveness . . . anyone. God will manifest his presence. God will listen and draw near (1 Kings 8:29–30). His house is also a place of justice and compassion, where victims are vindicated and perpetrators are found out. It is a place where perpetrators come to ask and receive forgiveness, to learn repentance as a new way of life. It is the place where the sinned against wrestle to forgive and to take bitterness out with the wash and to leave it there. Farmers in drought, the ravaged in famine, the heart in affliction, the defeated soldier in battle, the Israelite in time of need, the Gentile foreigner who seeks God; the house of God is a house of prayer for all of these neighbors. No one is kept out of God's house by his or her sin. On the contrary, it is sin and affliction under the sun that bid them come and enter in order to confess and find forgiveness, to seek and to learn, to find mercy and aid in relationship with God (1 Kings 8:22–53).

For many of us, as we have mentioned, God houses do not carry these kinds of connotations. God humbly demonstrates his majestic power for our good out of gracious love in the context of all that perplexes us, and breaks us, including our neighbors and our enemies, in our sins under the sun. In contrast, churches have sometimes offered nothing more than man-made walls filled with political maneuvering, relational rancor, cruel misjudgments, dismissing of questions, and pursuing forgiveness only for a select few after we get good enough to receive it. Some of us love it this way. We like the privileges it preserves for us, the lifestyles and the deference for which we use it. For others, a house of God is boredom draped in trite sayings, carpeted with irrelevance, and painted with the pretensions of the seething who smile and the clueless who trite us with nice sayings; Bible verses and church-sign quotes pulled out like the fortunes found in our after-lunch cookies down at the Chinese buffet; greeting cards of religion stamped in cursive and mailed at holidays and crutch times.

But now we begin to demonstrate why the Preacher doesn't choose to dismiss church. Jesus takes this approach and establishes it. In his zeal, Jesus cries out against the misuse of God's house. Each of us hears the whip cracked and sees our table overturned.

And he was teaching them and saying to them, "Is it not written, 'My house shall be called a house of prayer for all the nations'? But you have made it a den of robbers." (Mark 11:17)

In Jesus' day, "all the nations" were not allowed; if they were, it was only by segregation into classes of people only capable of worship at lesser and greater places within the building, like those divided into first and second class on an airplane. People made money off the poor. They sold goods needed for sacrifices and profited from what God himself had required and provided. Commercial or competitive use rather than prayer was the norm.

Perhaps now we can recognize the irritation and the connection. What Solomon prays and preaches concerning the house of God, Jesus passionately recovers. To Jesus, the house of God is not a house of commerce or power for clergy. Neither is it a house without forgiveness, open only to those who can prove their status, demonstrate their worth, or gain enough clout to get in. God's house has his name on it not ours, no matter how much money we've given for its use. God's house is a place of prayer, a place where God draws near to listen to the plight of human beings under the sun with their lot and their seasons, their disquiets and their delights. A neighbor from any nation (and we must by grace come to terms with this); whether that neighbor be a man or woman, child or adult, rich or poor, they are meant to have access to this house of God. How else could we presume to access it ourselves except through pride, and we are told plainly that God opposes the proud (James 4:6).

Access is granted, not on the basis of whom one knows, or what one wears, or what color of skin, or how much of the Bible is familiar, or the political party or denomination to which one belongs. Access is granted on the basis of a sacrifice for sin that God himself ordained and provided and that we ourselves without him could never have attained (1 Kings 8:62–64).

And there it is. The purpose for the house is prayer for us and for our neighbors on the basis of God's sacrificial love. This purpose exposes the basis for our presence at the house and the basis for God's presence with us at the house. Access to the house of God has required a prior provision from God. Otherwise, none of us could enter. Mercy undergirds every step we take down the aisle. Grace defends every time we sit within the seat or lean against the wall. The lamb slain pays for our sins and secures access every time we presume to open the door. Maybe that is what we must remember. We could never presume to enter the house of God—and this includes Solomon the king, the Jewish son of the Messiah's lineage—unless God himself paid for what our accounts could not sustain. No matter how many pews we have purchased, how long our family has been in the congregation, how true our doctrinal statements, how packed our houses, or what roles we have fulfilled, these all disintegrate into eraser dust. Only by the Lamb that was slain can one enter this temple, no matter who he or she is and no matter how those who decide worth under the sun regard them.

> Then the king, and all Israel with him, offered sacrifice before the LORD. Solomon offered as peace offerings to the LORD 22,000 oxen and 120,000 sheep. So the king and all the people of Israel dedicated the house of the LORD. (1 Kings 8:62–63)

So, "when" we go to the house of God, we do so amid the delightful and disquieting seasons that are ours under this broiling yellow orb. All around the church doors, jokes, alcohol, art, nature, money and possessions, music, sex, affirmation, and work abound in all their nobility and temptations to misuse. God sets up a confession booth in the midst. But he wants us to listen when we come in. He has things to confess about himself. But what he has to confess isn't his sin. Instead, he declares that he created you with purpose to know him and to enjoy him. He created a house as a place in the broken world where we can come and he will recover wisdom and grace again. He lets us know that he will not allow the foolish works of churchgoing harmers to last. He lets us know that he is not naive regarding what people do in his name. He declares that he has an alternative way of life that opposes the wreckage. He invites us to healing. He calms our hearts and quiets our voices. We learn again to discern echoes of Eden, the voice that it is his. Grace is ours. He gives it freely. One greater than Solomon is here.

CONCLUSION

Imagine a scene on the steps of a hospital. A man has recently fled there from the emergency room. What he sees in the emergency room tosses his stomach and draws sweat to his brow and palms. He needs air. He needs to sit down. As he tries to recover himself, a woman walks briskly past him toward the door. He staggers out of his shock and urgently tries to stop her. "Wait!" he yells. "Don't open those doors! Don't you know what goes on in there?"

She pauses and turns toward him. He sees now that she is wearing a surgeon's gear. "Yes," she says calmly and with empathy. "Yes, sir. I do." Then, after pausing a moment to discern and to settle whether or not he needs further attention, she turns, opens the doors, and moves purposefully inside.

When the Preacher urges us to guard our steps when we enter God's house, he indicates for us who need air that he knows what goes on when one opens those doors and steps inside. But the Preacher's view of church leads him neither to ignore its necessity nor to mask its difficulties. He does not sentimentalize church but neither does he abandon it. "Under the sun, when you open the church doors," he says, "you have to watch your step."

165

QUESTIONS FOR DISCUSSION

1. What do you think about the idea that sometimes church can make atheists of us?
2. Describe the qualities of a foolish churchgoer. What about these qualities tempts you?
3. Describe the qualities of the wise churchgoer. What grace do you need in order to grow in this direction?
4. What is the purpose of the house of God? How has Jesus provided for this purpose?
5. What provision has Jesus made for the foolish and the wise churchgoer?

CHAPTER NINE

KEPT OCCUPIED BY GOD

"I need Thee every hour; stay Thou nearby."[1]

"The Questions Our Young People Are Asking."

This title identified a series of sermons that my associate pastors and I once preached. We invited those in junior and senior high anonymously to ask questions about God and about life. Then, each Sunday morning we tried to begin an answer to one of those questions.

One such question raised a tension and a frustration that most of us who follow Jesus have experienced. "Why is it that when I'm at church or at youth group or at summer camp," one young person asked, "I experience God in a powerful way. But then when I go back into my week of homework, practice, chores, and stuff, I lose God? Nothing changes the everyday. How do I get God into my everyday life?"

This is an important question, and the Preacher seems to have something like this on his mind. He has just taken us into the house of God. There, he has shown us how God intends to meet with us. Now he walks out of the church doors with us. He pauses with us and has us take a look around. The "under the sun" world didn't transform itself into heaven between the time we entered and exited our meeting with God in the sanctuary. The house of God is no rabbit's foot or genie bottle that when rubbed makes the bad things go away.

167

The Preacher takes us from God's house in Ecclesiastes 5 back into the world again. Standing there outside the church doors, the Preacher uses the rest of Ecclesiastes 5, 6, 7, and on through to the rest of his message as binoculars through which to survey the world as it continues on while God's people go in and out of his house. The Preacher tells us there in front of the church doors that even though we've been inside with God, and this for the marvelous sanity of our souls, evil still remains under this sun and human beings still live beneath the heavy burden of it all (Eccl. 5:13, 16; 6:1; 9:3; 10:13). Abuses among rich and poor, misuses of money, folk wisdoms that misguide us, relational damage between men and women, calamity and foolish leaders, still kick our shins and laugh at the bruising.

This fact can dishearten us. No wonder the young person asked the question. We all empathize with it. We taste God's presence and then go back into a world that seems bent on souring heavenly tastes. We leave the mountaintop only to enter the valley again. It seems that God gets lost to us. In this light, I wonder how Lazarus, the man that Jesus raised from the dead, handled this reality? After all, though he experienced healing from Jesus, Lazarus reentered a community only to receive death threats on his life (John 12:10). Or what about the Samaritan woman who kissed Jesus' feet and experienced Jesus' grace, love, and forgiveness in the Pharisee's house (Luke 7:36–50)? She knew Jesus now, and yet when she walked down the street that night under the sun, she was still a Samaritan, still a woman, and in the eyes of many, still a scandal of a human being. Why go to church if going to church doesn't change the world? Why go to the house of God if when we come back out of its doors during the day we still have to lock ours at night?

The Preacher seems to partially answer this question first by an ongoing and sober statement of something sadly true. Churchgoers have no immunity under the sun. Forgiven sinners and freed tomb dwellers will have happen to them what happens to anyone in the fallen world. This is worth lamenting. We call this what it is. This lack of immunity the Preacher teaches us to call an "evil" that remains under the sun (Eccl. 9:3). No wonder we lose our sense of God sometimes when church ends and the workaday world begins. We can follow the Preacher's lead on this and learn to talk honestly about this with our neighbors.

But the question still remains. How do we maintain a sense of God when we leave church? "No immunity" offers part of an answer in that it affirms that our experience of loss is not unique or strange to human beings under the sun. But this affirmation offers very little joy or hope. So, there on the church steps with our binoculars, the Preacher tells us to look and see something frustratingly mysterious and marvelously profound. "Though a sinner does evil a hundred times and prolongs his life," the Preacher insists, "yet I know that it will be well with those who fear God, because they fear before him" (Eccl. 8:12). Immunity does not exist, but intimacy and well-being do. Furthermore, among the evils that remain, the Preacher wants to insist that God possesses a power that he gives to his people to enjoy God. God intimately enters these evils in order to keep us occupied joyfully with him all the days that we live (Eccl. 5:19, 20; 6:2).

In sum, God doesn't just meet with us in his house, he also meets with us in his world. If that is true, then exactly how does God find us and grant us a sense of him in our ordinary lives amid our homework, chores, and stuff? In this chapter, we will seek to find out. First, what are the evils that church attendance will not change and that make our sense of God in this world so difficult? Second, we return to the theme of joy that God nonetheless gives us the power to experience.

MONEY IS A HARD THING

Money and possessions are mixed up with one of the evils that make it hard for us to relate to God outside of the church doors in the everyday. The One greater than Solomon would mince no words on this subject. "The deceitfulness of riches" is like a farmer's good seeds sown among thorns. The thorns, like riches, "choke the word" of God in one's life. Surrounded by fields and fields of money and possessions, the warehouses of the soul remain empty and barren, unable to offer any fruit to another (Matt. 13:22).

The Preacher wants us to come out of God's house and then recognize locations in which the poor are oppressed by money-grubbers, and this with no just remedy. The plight of the poor is made worse as their rights are also trampled upon (Eccl. 5:8). These conditions take place when middle managers, CEOs, and government officials each get caught up in power structures, which serve the bottom line of financial production and gain. These leaders and brokers have their own jobs on the line if they are not able to report to their higher-ups an ongoing increase in revenue. "For the high official is watched by a higher, and there are yet higher ones over them" (Eccl. 5:8). In such a system, the ordinary worker gets used and misused in order to keep the dollar signs from falling. In contrast, how blessed the workers are when a king resists such greed and control and remains "committed to cultivated fields" (Eccl. 5:9). Likely, the Preacher says this because in Israel cultivated fields within a community of just and fair labor meant that the poor, the widow, and the stranger were cared for while the worker and the fruit of his labor were protected (Lev. 19:10; 23:22). In contrast, Israel had known what it was to have leaders who used whips, gave them no straw, but demanded more bricks and in less time (Ex. 5:7–14).

There on the steps of the house of God, we are not meant to "be amazed" at this situation (Eccl. 5:8). Instead, the Preacher shows us how to give language and empathy to the unjust conditions in which such neighbors find themselves. Going to the house of God and discerning God in the everyday when one has no rights and no remedy from an oppressor who cares only about the money produced rather than the life lived is a difficult burden to bear.

The Preacher also wants us to come out of God's house and then recognize the neighbor who must try to make sense of God in his work amid his "vexation and sickness and anger" (Eccl. 5:17). This kind of "darkness" shrouds the neighbor's life because he made poor business decisions or gambled his money away or, like a faithful worker with years of dedication to the company whose managers stole or lost his retirement, this neighbor was painfully swindled out of his money. Either way, his "riches were lost in a bad venture" (Eccl. 5:14). The result is that this neighbor has no financial means to help his children. "He is father of a son, but he has nothing in hand" (Eccl. 5:13). These parents and children have to try and relate to God beneath this daily strain for having enough food, clothing, and sustenance. If they come to the house of God, these neighbors do so with no financial security and no fruit to enjoy from the work they do each day (Eccl. 5:15–16). This neighbor will work and work with no opportunity for financial relief all his days. How does a person discern God when each day vexes, sickens, or embitters him?

As a pastor over the years, I have sat a handful of times across from men whose riches were lost to them and who then wondered whether their lives were worth living at all. Equally evil and difficult is the man, who in contrast to these impoverished or bad-ventured neighbors, has everything the world can offer and yet has no joy with God in them. Such a person neither recognizes gratefully that such good things come from God in his grace nor sees that such things are meant by God to pleasantly provide for our own and another's joy (Eccl. 6:1–2). Such a man "fathers a hundred children and lives many years, so that the days of his years are many, but his soul is not satisfied with life's good things" (Eccl. 6:3).

TWO ANALOGIES

The Preacher uses two analogies to show the emptiness of the wealthy neighbor who does not know God and does not discern God's joy in the good things God gives him. The first analogy uses hyperbole to picture a man with more kids than one can imagine and who lives a long and happy life. This neighbor possesses everything valued in that time and place—a full quiver of heirs, a long legacy, and family wealth in the world. Yet, the Preacher points out, this person in truth "has no burial" (Eccl. 6:3). This phrase often designates judgment and isolation from the benefits of true piety and community.[2] Jesus took up this theme by telling a story, which featured a rich man who stored up his wealth but not his soul (Luke 12:13–21).

"Soul," the wealthy man says to himself, "you have ample goods laid up for many years; relax, eat, drink, be merry" (Luke 12:19).

Then, reminiscent of the Preacher who warns that "a stranger enjoys" these gifts rather than the one to whom they were given (Eccl. 6:2), Jesus goes on with the story. "But God said to him, 'Fool! This night your soul is required of you, and the things you have prepared, whose will they be?'" (Luke 12:20).

Then Jesus declares the moral of his story. "So is the one who lays up treasure for himself and is not rich toward God" (Luke 12:21).

Then, the second analogy used by the Preacher startles us. "I say that a stillborn child is better off than" the rich man who has no joy in God. "For it comes in vanity and goes in darkness, and in darkness its name is covered" (Eccl. 6:3–4).

> Moreover, it has not seen the sun or known anything, yet it finds rest rather than he. Even though he should live a thousand years twice over, yet enjoy no good—do not all go to the one place? (Eccl. 6:5–6)

For those who have miscarried children, this verse can wound or frighten at first glance. It can seem to us that the Preacher speaks without human sensitivity to our pains. It can also seem that the Preacher is theologically inaccurate by speaking as if there is no heaven or light or comfort for such a child, only darkness. But a closer reading reminds us that the Preacher is using poetry to expose the deep fallacy in the godless wealthy man's thinking. Those who love wealth and do not derive from God the pleasure intended in God believe that they are blessed among men and have achieved everything a person could desire. In contrast, the worst possible life, according to this way of thinking, is the one that barely got started and never got to possess or attain these earthly treasures. "How sad," such a person would say.

But the Preacher turns this view on its head. The still-born child, though he or she never had money, never built a house, never saw the latest movies or tried on the latest trends, is nonetheless, at rest. Rest, and this with God, is one thing the rich man still does not possess. "His soul is not satisfied with life's good things" (Eccl. 6:3). For all of his wealth, he possesses no contentment. Restless and unfamiliar with true joy, the wealthy neighbor is impoverished. The stillborn child possesses the riches of rest and provision with God that the wealthy neighbor knows nothing of. No wonder Jesus teaches us that it is hard for a rich man to discern, enjoy, and embrace the kingdom of God (Matt. 19:24).

TWO TREASURES

In contrast to those who gain wealth through oppression and those who gain wealth honestly but without God, there is a kind of rest and contentment with God that aligns with the child who, to our minds, died too early. It reveals itself in the sweetness of sleep that an honest laborer experiences each night, "whether he eats little or much." In contrast, the rich without God is up at night because of his wealth and what it takes to keep it (Eccl. 5:12). It aligns itself with the honest worker whom God has given wealth but who knows that this gift from God does not overshadow what is true and lasting—accepting our lot, giving thanks for the food we have, and finding joy in our daily work. Such a person, whose joy is in God, "will not much remember the days of his life because God keeps him occupied with joy in his heart" (Eccl. 5:18–20). There in the world, God and a human being, under the sun, can still find pleasure in each other's company. Such persons have believed and trusted the point of view that admits that "he who loves money will not be satisfied with money, nor he who loves wealth with his income. . . . When goods increase, they increase who eat them" (Eccl. 5:10–11). Rest of soul, contentment, and gratitude are not tied to how little or how much a person gains. For this reason, there is hope, however little it seems under the sun, for the oppressed, the poor, the bad-ventured, and the ordinary worker.

This view of true and lasting treasure does not rise uniquely from the Preacher's mind. The sage tradition upon which the Preacher stands makes this contrast of treasures plain.

"It is better to be of a lowly spirit with the poor than to divide the spoil with the proud." (Prov. 16:19)

"Better is a poor person who walks in his integrity than one who is crooked in speech and is a fool." (Prov. 19:1)

"What is desired in a man is steadfast love, and a poor man is better than a liar." (Prov. 19:22)

"Better is a poor man who walks in his integrity than a rich man who is crooked in his ways." (Prov. 28:6)

Jesus fulfills this teaching when he exposes treasures as divided into two kinds—those which rust and those which do not (Matt. 6:19–20). He graciously invites us to that which provides contentment, rest, and joy with God when he makes plain the implications of these two kinds of treasures. "No one can serve two masters" (Matt. 6:24). Various neighbors feel the burden that money and our misuses of it bring. Discerning God in our poverty or in our wealth impacts the conditions of what kinds of folks will walk into the house of God. Money makes it hard to keep God in our sight during the ordinary of every day. However, grace, joy, and contentment with God even under this wearying sun are not made void.

THE PREACHER'S APPROACH
TO MIXED MESSAGES

In high school, I participated in a play entitled *Rashomon*. The play and movie derived their plots from two short stories written by Japanese author Ryunosuke Akutagawa. In response to a crime, four witnesses offer equally plausible but definitively contrary explanations of what happened. A priest must listen to four differing accounts of the event offered by a bandit, a samurai, the samurai's wife, and a woodcutter. Perplexed and confounded, the priest begins to lose hope. What is true and good has lost. Only lies, deceptions, mixed messages, and selfish spin remain. In the end, however, the priest discovers that the confusion of mixed voices has not eradicated beauty and truth.

Mixed messages also make it difficult for us to find God in our daily lives. The Preacher takes us out of the house of God in Ecclesiastes 5, into the misuse of money and people in Ecclesiastes 6, and on into the kinds of messages in Ecclesiastes 7 that we have to disregard or embrace under the sun each day. He does this in Ecclesiastes 7 by turning our attention to a series of proverbs.

These proverbs expose the kind of assumptions within us that drive us to oppress others or to pursue money without God or to sink down in bitterness from our bad ventures and impoverished conditions.

At halftime of the big game the athlete who has played poorly and unwisely will not hear his coach say things like, "No need to concentrate, let's get a six pack and some women and forget about it; who cares, take a look through this book of jokes; let's tell some, have a party, and laugh till it hurts all night." On the contrary, with the game on the line, and everything they've worked and trained for slipping through their fingers, not because they've played their best and can't win, but because they are playing foolishly and losing, the coach will frown and cry out, "Focus! Is that you laughing over there, Jones? This ain't no time to smile! You want to laugh like it's party time? Well, you can walk on out that door right now! I need a team that has guts and is willing to get down to business. Willis, is that you cracking jokes back there?! Get your head in this game, son! That team out there is destroying you! You want to tell jokes, you can walk on out that door! I need a team that knows that we are better than this! Do you feel that burning in your chest? You feel that ache of defeat and intimidation and regret creeping into you, staring you down? Don't ignore that ache! Don't make friends with it and ask it out for a drink! Look it square in the face! It has come to own you. Don't let it! Learn from it. Cry about it, yell at it, whatever you need to do to take a look at this moment in your life and to realize this is it! This ain't no recess. This ain't practice. There is no other game. It's time to get serious then! Twenty more minutes to lay your heart and soul on the line and give it every serious effort you've got!"

When you begin to read this list of proverbs in Ecclesiastes 7, you see that the Preacher is doing something like this coach. He says things that seem to disparage laughter, celebrating with friends, and mirth. As you hear him remember two things.

1. This Preacher commends joy. We have already discovered his intentional repetition of our hope for God's gift of joy in our ordinary lot, our relationships, seasons, our work, and our food. He is certainly not a stoic or a religious fussbudget who refuses glad-hearted belly laughs and good times.
2. This Preacher has the various evils under the sun on his mind. We know this because of everything we have been reading and hearing from him thus far. With oppression, misuse, bitterness, and death roaming about under the sun, and seemingly defeating us, the Preacher recalls us to the seriousness and focus required.

And so the Preacher of joy keeps our gaze upon that which breaks us under the sun. Remember, he is not yelling. His face isn't red, nor are his eyes full of bombast or anger. In this way, the moment resembles halftime, but the Preacher's approach resembles very little how coaches generally motivate players. He is like a server who puts a full meal on our table, slides it in front of us, looks us in the eyes, and deliberately says calmly, "Watch out, this plate is hot." Don't let these calm words of poetic speech lull us into disregard for them. If we touch the plate without care it will burn us. Make no mistake. These words are full of nourishment, yes, but also full of heat. When we walk outside of the church doors, mixed messages and money pressures assail us. No wonder hearing God in the ordinary challenges us.

OUR DISCERNMENT OF MIXED MESSAGES

To begin, we are told under the sun and in our hearts that material possessions are more valuable than the content of our character and the qualities of our souls. We sell ourselves and give ourselves away for trinkets, like Esau giving away his birthright to Jacob just to satisfy his momentary hunger. But the Preacher holds on to the truth that "a good name is better than precious ointment" (Eccl. 7:1). Under the sun, a faithful and humble person might get overlooked or dishonored in favor of those who possess the glamour that sparkles under the sun. Being overlooked by precious-ointment buyers and sellers under the sun can make it feel as if God is not with us in the everyday. Their voices can seemingly drown out his. So, the Preacher puts voice again to the sound of wisdom.

We are also told under the sun that this life is all there is and that death brings an end to everything good, true, and meaningful. But the Preacher declares that "the day of death [is better] than the day of birth" (Eccl. 7:1). Solomon could mean this in light of his previous statements (Eccl. 4:3; 6:3). Death holds an analogy to those who, in contrast to restless neighbors who scour for life without God under the sun, have true rest and deliverance from it all. Most likely, however, the placement of a "good name" and "precious ointment" corresponds in the proverb to the day of death and birth. Birth is like precious ointment, sweet smelling, wonderful in itself, and holding out a promise for rejuvenation. But precious ointment doesn't reveal character. Just as an evil person can use precious ointment, so one's birth does not indicate the kind of person one is and will become. Death reveals the life that preceded it. The end of a person's life offers a more sure measure of the person than its beginnings. "Better is the end of a thing than its beginning" (Eccl. 7:8). It is the obituary not the birth announcement that best reveals the measure of a person. Endings tell us more than beginnings can. Furthermore, the death we see in our neighbors tells us about our future, "for this is the end of all mankind" (Eccl. 7:2). The sooner we come to terms with our death, the wiser our life has the chance to become. Our death informs our prayers and our life.

O Lord, make me know my end
　　and what is the measure of my days;
　　let me know how fleeting I am! . . .
And now, O Lord, for what do I wait?
　　My hope is in you. (Ps. 39:4, 7)

We who avoid our purpose as death reveals it because we fear our death are given profound grace and empowerment in Jesus, the One greater than Solomon. He delivers us from the fear of dying so that in him, we might rise from our bondage and live purposed in him (Heb. 2:15).

Another mixed message that calls out to us under the sun and makes it hard to discern God in our lives tells us that an unexamined life built on constant distraction and the pursuit of momentary pleasures will make us wise and happy. The Preacher says otherwise. His concern is that while we live, we learn to look at reality under the sun and "lay it to heart" (Eccl. 7:2). The sage Preacher calls for human beings to contemplate what it means that life is the way it is. More often we do "not ponder the path of life." Our "ways wander" and we do "not know it" (Prov. 5:6). "Ponder," then, "the path of your feet; then all your ways will be sure" (Prov. 4:26).

Distraction constitutes the primary means by which we resist a contemplative way of life. Distraction comes in at least two forms. The first uses disquiet to distract us. These persons go constantly to the house of mourning and sorrow, not because their season of pain warrants it, nor because depression has picked a fight with them, but because they choose lament as a way to do life regardless of the season. Such a person talks often of the funeral home but never "lays it to heart." This person is always sad but never learning what sadness in God's wise and kind hands is meant to teach us and to point us toward. This use of mourning has an amnesia to it. We forget that we are, in the Preacher's words, "the living" (Eccl. 7:2). We are not dead. "The living" have an active purpose and calling yet

179

before them. "The living" engage God and this life each day and they "lay it to heart." Wisdom does not use sad things to avoid life. Wisdom uses sad things to learn life. "By sadness of face the heart is made glad" (Eccl. 7:3). The Preacher doesn't say that it is better to be sad. He says that it is better to engage sadness and to take to heart what it has to teach us who live.

In contrast, the other distraction uses delights to avoid laying things to heart. These persons avoid the house of mourning. Mirth, laughter, and the house of feasting form their constant choice or even addiction each day. But the Preacher recalls for us that two kinds of laughter, song, mirth, and feasting exist under the sun, just as there are two kinds of treasure.

This contrast is made most clear in Ecclesiastes 7:3. There is a kind of laughter that is not best for us. "Sorrow is better than laughter." Yet there is a kind of profound gladness that we can nonetheless experience. "The heart is made glad." One kind of happiness the Preacher identifies as "the heart of fools," "the song of fools," "the laughter of the fools." This kind of mirth is like "the crackling of thorns under a pot" (Eccl. 7:4-6). The pot looks whole. The plant stands tall. The image delights. But lift the pot and your fingers will bleed. Thorns are there hidden within the beauty. The pot is actually broken. The chipped holes lie beneath its surface. Soon enough, water will not hold and what now blooms will wither away. Some of us are laughing and singing, but we've never learned the kind of gladness in God that the sad who have laid such things to heart have come to daily and sweetly and deeply taste. The Preacher, then, doesn't stand at a distance and mock the foolish. Instead, he beckons us for our good to consider the kind of gladness that can satisfy our being. He believes this exists. He himself seems to have known it. Desiring our good under the sun, he calls us to seek such gladness.

This longing for our good exposes why the Preacher also challenges those mixed messages within our culture which urge us to sexualize relationships. Such messages offer us friends with benefits. They offer us a win-win proposition for doing life among men and women. Using poetic language and exaggeration, the Preacher seeks to disrupt the damage that men and women do to each other sexually.

> And I find something more bitter than death: the woman whose heart is snares and nets, and whose hands are fetters. He who pleases God escapes her, but the sinner is taken by her. (Eccl. 7:26)

Like most poetic speech, a first glance is like trying to use a Styrofoam cup to dry a flooded basement or boat. There is too much water for a cup to hold. Buckets, large ones, are required, and this means making several trips to fill and empty. Poetic speech is like that. Our first glance at this verse can trouble us. But make several trips to its meaning and the waters subside, revealing the furniture that sits there. The trouble lessens as its meaning surfaces.

Notice first that the Preacher does not describe every woman or womankind. He has in mind one particular brand of woman who possesses a particular condition of heart. "The woman whose heart is snares and nets." Something has happened to this woman and she has quit on love. Or she lusts to exalt herself and to feel what it means to have the notice of men. Either way, whether temporarily or as a way of life, she uses her body and words to get the notice of a man and to set a trap for him so that he takes to her.

Notice also that the Preacher does not exclude men. While there are men whose hearts are snares and nets and we might wish that he made it plainer that he knows this, he also quietly exposes a certain brand of man too. Not all men, not mankind, but the kind of man whose heart can be "taken by her." There is a kind of woman who does not care whether she or the man she wants is married.

181

The sexual power that God gave her to use in the context of fidelity and love to the man she would marry is used instead to seduce a certain kind of man. She cares only for the money or the moment. She consumes rather than loves. Likewise, there is a kind of man whose sexual power was meant to gift, empower, and bless the woman with whom he would covenant. But he too imagines what is illusory and takes hold of wind in the name of intimacy or love or companionship. He consumes rather than loves. Mutual misuse isn't love. It is as if this kind of man and this kind woman say to each other, "Let's do something to each other that isn't loving. Let's use one another and make no commitments or demands or expectations that tomorrow we will honor one another with care, sacrifice, or love." They both agree. The Preacher believes that neighbors using one another for their own lust or gain damages people. He upholds love for neighbor as his abiding assumption. By using this kind of language, the Preacher follows the sage tradition of poetically warning of the death, bitterness, and disillusionment that men and women who choose adultery, sexual misuse, and one-night stands ultimately bring upon themselves and their neighbors (Prov. 2:16–19; 7:6–27). For those of us who have grasped this kind of wind and felt its emptiness, we affirm the wisdom and care of the Preacher's words. Worn out with use, we too now long for sex and relationship between a man and woman in the way it was meant to be in the context of cherishing and respecting each other in true fidelity and covenant love. As it is, we hardly know what it is like be looked at or touched by the opposite sex without them using us with their eyes or gaming us with their words.

At this point, the Preacher cautions us against self-righteousness. "Surely there is not a righteous man on earth who does good and never sins" (Eccl. 7:20). The Preacher is not only concerned with a certain kind of woman, but he is also not afraid to plainly expose men, even those who are "righteous" in their ways. Such a man does not

commit adultery or pay a prostitute but that his sin finds
him out in multiple other ways. The Preacher's longing to
defend neighbors from sexual misuse does not lull him
to hypocrisy in his preaching regarding other kinds of
neighbors and our sins.

Because of this, we who try to act righteously ought
to watch out for being too easily or naively offended. "Do
not take to heart all the things that people say, lest you
hear your servant cursing you." Why? Because "your heart
knows that many times you yourself have cursed others"
(Eccl. 7:21–22).

TRYING TO FIGURE THINGS OUT

This is part of what happens to us as we seek a contemplative life among the mixed messages. Ours becomes
a vocation of meditation among the action. We look at life
the way we read a poem, humbly and slowly. We cannot
get the meaning the first time around or the second. We
have to bring our buckets back and forth daily. We consider
what we see, gradually "adding one thing to another to
find the scheme of things," seeking with our soul "repeatedly" to turn our hearts "to know and to search out and
to seek wisdom and the scheme of things," to "know the
wickedness of folly and the foolishness that is madness"
(Eccl. 7:25–28). As we learn to approach each day like
this, we begin to recognize ourselves in the foolish things
that others do. The Preacher has told us in Ecclesiastes 5
that the problems under the sun reside within the church
doors. Now he tells us that those under-the-sun problems
reside with us.

In fact, line up one thousand men, and only one of
them will approximate the wisdom we need under the
sun. Even if that line of one thousand men consisted all
of churchgoers and the masculine "righteous." Still, it is a
large crowd of illusion, for nine hundred ninety-nine of us

righteous ones would be exposed for our thoroughgoing folly (Eccl. 7:28). At this point, we are humbled or relieved to see Solomon push back on religious pretense, masculine arrogance, and the hypocrisy of both.

Harder to understand is what he seems to imply next. If he finds one man in a thousand who is without folly, "a woman among all these I have not found" (Eccl. 7:28). Poetically, the Preacher is using a metaphor to state that out of a group of two thousand men and women, only one person would likely possess the contemplative wisdom and the true kind of joy that we were created to experience. And yet, even that person is a sinner (Eccl. 7:20). At this point, what Solomon says makes sense. But why does he identify the person as a man and suggest plainly that if he only finds one man that is wise, he has not found one woman in that same crowd? After all, the Preacher has made the beauty and dignity of women clear elsewhere in his message (Eccl. 9:9). The sage tradition in which Solomon speaks readily commends and identifies the ready existence and blessing of wise women (Prov. 31).

Two interpretations seem probable.

One, we simply do not know how to rightly interpret Solomon's poetry. Earlier cultures agreed with the seeming disparagement toward women. Our culture disagrees with the seeming disparagement toward women. Perhaps we confess our cultural noise. We state what we know for sure that it cannot mean and we stop there, recognize the limits of what seems fuzzy to us, and wait upon God for the sentence that troubles us and shouldn't or doesn't trouble us and should.

Two, we take Solomon seriously when he tells us about his personal experience. Solomon had first-hand experience with foolish men and on occasion he met a wise man such as Nathan the prophet. But Solomon's choice of women was unfortunate. He surrounded himself, not with women of the covenant for whom the fear of God anchored their heart and pursuit in life. Instead, Solomon "had a thousand wives and concubines in his royal harem—unbelieving women who worshipped foreign gods (see 1 Kings 11:3)" and who possessed little access to the wisdom found in the God of Israel. "The Bible says that these women turned Solomon away to the worship of other gods (see 1 Kings 11:1–8)."[3] If the Preacher is testifying to what he learned after his downfall, then it makes sense why this section about sex, men, and women possesses a more passionate use of metaphor ("more bitter than death," Eccl. 7:26) than perhaps other sections in his message.

Similarly, in a male-dominated society in which the education of women depended upon upright men, women found themselves at a terrible disadvantage. The Preacher implies this disadvantage. When only one out of a thousand is found to possess wisdom, those who must depend upon others for their education are left to learn by perusing libraries of folly. If so, Solomon's remarks are sadly factual rather than sarcastically disparaging. Impoverished women exist in large part because of the fault of men in a society of male-dominated foolishness. Because of this, his point remains regarding the human condition. Wise humanity describes a rare thing.

Either way, the point Solomon makes is that uprightness and wisdom reflect the character of God. But we are hard pressed to find one human being who shows us this fact and even the one we might find is still a sinner. By saying such a thing, the Preacher includes himself. He too is a sinner who expresses a great deal of tragic folly. Consequently, he looks at men, women, and himself, surrounded and tempted by all of these mixed messages, and concludes: "See, this alone I found, that God made man upright, but they have sought out many schemes" (Eccl. 7:29).

TWO KINDS OF STRATEGIES

In the Saint Louis area where I live, two relatives, an uncle and a nephew, argued in the backyard. Both were standing by the grill, cooking pork for the family. The uncle named the pork they were cooking "pork chops." The nephew disagreed. "They are called 'pork steaks,' " he insisted. The argument heated like the grill. It ended that night. The nephew walked into the living room and shot his uncle dead. The nephew was right. The uncle had been foolish and wrong in his naming of the thing. The meats on the grill were indeed properly called "pork steaks." But the means the nephew used to respond to his uncle's folly was more foolish than the first. Death came because of a disagreement over what to call dinner.[4]

Amid all of these evils under the sun, we are tempted to use folly to fight folly. The Preacher admits this. "Oppression drives the wise into madness." We get worn out with mixed messages. The kinds of promises, songs, mirth, and laughter that oppressors indulge in with their thorn-laden beauties look so appealing and seem so wise and helpful. We get frustrated or tired or despairing. We join in. But "a bribe corrupts the heart" even of the wise, and we too can lose our way (Eccl. 7:7).

We know that we are using folly as a strategy to overcome folly when impatient pride, hasty anger, or naive nostalgia forms our weapon of choice to shake us free from the mixed messages. The so-called "wise ones" who follow God begin to believe that if they just act now, get loud, and denounce all things current in favor of the good old days, then all will go well with us. But the Preacher insists that impatient pride, hasty anger, or naive nostalgia only make things worse. Why?

"Because the patient in spirit is better than the proud of spirit" (Eccl. 7:8). The grace of wisdom does not fight pride with more pride. If both teams turn out the lights, no one can see. "Everyone who exalts himself will be humbled," Jesus insisted. "Everyone" includes the follower of God and the one who is right about how pork on a grill should be named. No matter who we are or how right we may be, God does not exalt pride. In contrast, "the one who humbles himself will be exalted" (Luke 18:14).

Because "anger lodges in the heart of fools" (Eccl. 7:9). Anger acts like an addictive drug. Each time we use it, its chemicals work to further our dependence upon them. Anger begins to take up residence within us and becomes part and parcel of our being. Anger begins to own us. We lose our ability to live without it. When Samaritans rudely dismissed Jesus, James and John wanted to respond quickly and with anger. "Lord, do you want us to tell fire to come down from heaven and consume them?" But Jesus "turned and rebuked them. And they went on to another village" (Luke 9:54–56).

Because, "it is not from wisdom" that we propose that "the former days [were] better than these" (Eccl. 7:10). The Preacher has already established that "nothing new" takes place under the sun (Eccl. 1:9). What is has been. Humility recognizes this truth that we are no different in heart, season, and calamity than those who have come before us. We do now what they did then, only we express our scheming hearts in different forms. The "good old days" are lyrics found in the songs of fools, myths among the stories that fools tell each other. When followers of Jesus experienced hardship, misuse, and betrayal because they followed Jesus, Jesus answered, "Rejoice in that day, and leap for joy, for behold, your reward is great in heaven." And then he adds why. "For so their fathers did to the prophets" (Luke 6:23). Hard-heartedness is like a baton in a race that each runner passes on to the next. At the end of the race, though each runner ran a different portion, they all carried the same baton. So it is with each generation of human beings under the sun.

Pride, anger, naiveté, and nostalgia are like Stalin's communists waiting to deliver Poland out of the hands of Hitler's Nazis. What looks like a rescue only recovers and repeats the oppression. When God's people walk out of God's house and respond to the folly they find under the sun by becoming foolish themselves, there is little wonder why it can seem that God is nowhere to be found in the news, our neighborhoods, or our daily toil. We become like firefighters who, upon entering a burning building, disdain the water hoses and instead turn confidently to blowtorches and try helplessly to douse what blazes.

FINDING GOD OUTSIDE
THE CHURCH DOORS

No wonder the young person took us pastors up on our offer to ask a question! No wonder she wanted to find out how to maintain a sense of God when she leaves God's house and enters the sick soul of the broken-boned world. Daily life under the sun is infested with the loveless schemes of human beings. The character and purposes of God shine like an eclipsed sun, radiating light and heat hidden from view by what looks like dark shadow and feels like cold.

Beneath the shadows, what do you do? Start admitting your inabilities and instead throw your thoughts and affections in God's direction. You cannot fix most of what is broken. Unlike mechanical parts and unglued wood, the crooked parts of the people, the places, and the circumstances that you will encounter today are beyond your ability to repair. In contrast, the work of God constantly shows us that broken bones can dance again in him. For this reason, your main task each day is to learn how to contemplate each thing you experience in light of who God is and what God does. The Preacher says it this way: "Consider the work of God: who can make straight what he has made crooked?" (Eccl. 7:13). "Consider" means pay attention. You will want to lose focus. Or you will want to pay all of your attention to the works of men and women—scouring these human works beneath the dark and the shadow for a power big enough to make straight what breaks you and your neighbors. You can try this. God will let you. But it won't ultimately help you. Learn to pay attention to God. Turn your meditations to his work. Take your crooked things and set them in his presence.

How do you do this? Recognize the moment and respond accordingly. If something goes well in your day, no matter how small, celebrate over it! No more wondering if you can be happy about good things. No more needing to wait and pray to discover whether it is okay with God whether you smile or not. "In the day of prosperity be joyful" (Eccl. 7:14)! In college, when our team won a big game, our motto sounded something like this: "In the day of prosperity, get drunk and destroy stuff!" You may need to learn again what it means to truly celebrate something. God will teach you. Each day becomes full of small but genuine smiles when we take up joy in response to good things. A great deal of happiness is passing some of us by because we think that when a good thing happens we are supposed to consider it rather than get on with rejoicing over it.

In contrast, "in the day of adversity consider" (Eccl. 7:14). Let the tough stuff sink in. Don't run from it. Don't use god-talk to pretend it doesn't exist. Set your heart and mind on the awful thing. No evil thing can ultimately win. The foulest thing will reveal something true about the nature of life and the nobler purposes we were made for. Take time, lots of time, the time needed to grieve, ask questions, wrestle with it, work it out, and come to terms.

Why? Because though this is a mystery, we need to stand on this truth, that no matter what happens in our lives, God holds on to us and maintains his purposes for us. "God has made the one as well as the other, so that man may not find out anything that will be after him" (Eccl. 7:14). We cannot make crooked things straight. We can't fix everything. Now the Preacher humbles us to free us again by telling us that we can't know everything. A certain amount of ignorance attends everything we do— particularly when it comes to trying to figure out how it is that God governs and ordains both the good and the bad that happens in our lives and in the world. Solomon doesn't attempt to answer what we cannot know. Instead, he focuses on what we do know. Both good things and bad things happen to us. God is within the thing either way. This means that something larger than our prosperity and something larger than our adversity has a hold on us.

What does this mean? We get to lighten up. All our energy spent in trying to control and preserve our lives is next to worthless. "There is a righteous man who perishes in his righteousness, and there is a wicked man who prolongs his life in his evildoing" (Eccl. 7:15). There is no secret formula to life that if you could just figure it out or get in with God well enough, you could make everything happen the way you hope. It is time to relax your grip. The bargaining can stop. "Be not overly righteous, and do not make yourself too wise" (Eccl. 7:16). The whirlwind in your mind constantly trying to figure out everything in order to hold everything together is like chasing after the wind. We add wear and tear to our lives that God does not ask of us. "Why should you destroy yourself?" (Eccl. 7:16).

For others of us, we can stop acting as if, because we don't know everything and can't fix everything, nothing matters. We can stop with the excuses we use to justify the constant wandering and harm that we inflict on others and ourselves. God has the last word on our pain. God has the last word on our joy. Behind every pain, God is there letting nothing and no one separate us from him in Jesus. Behind every joy, God is there generously and graciously giving us something to rest happy about. So, "be not overly wicked, neither be a fool. Why should you die before your time?" (Eccl. 7:17).

How does this recognition of God's good governance over our prosperities and our adversities impact us? We fear less and try more things. No more being paralyzed by choices. We do our best to choose wisely. At the end of the day, whether we chose poorly or well, God will not leave us and will walk through it with us on to the other side and beyond. The

Preacher says it like this: "It is good that you should take hold of this, and from that withhold not your hand, for the one who fears God shall come out from both of them" (Eccl. 7:18).

In short, the Preacher gently teaches us about our practical atheisms. He shows us areas of control, self, and fear in the world that expose the ways we act as if God is not present. But according to the Preacher, there is nowhere we can go where God isn't already there. There is nowhere we can leave where God does not stay. Every bit of our skin, bone, thought, imagination, and feeling; every minute pleasure of our prosperity, every glass shard of our adversity; is held, governed, and seen through to us by God. Life under the sun is a God-inhabited life. The bent world rests and rebels within the arms of God.

The whole earth is full of his glory.

QUESTIONS FOR DISCUSSION

1. What from this chapter encouraged you? Unsettled you?
2. Why go to church if doing so doesn't change the world?
3. Why is money a hard thing? How does money tempt us to overlook true treasure?
4. What two kinds of distractions hinder a contemplative way of life?
5. Why does it not work to fight folly with folly? What kinds of folly are you tempted to choose when others treat you foolishly?
6. How do we come to terms with the Preacher's use of poetry regarding men, women, and wisdom?
7. How can we learn to find God outside of the church doors? What is a practical atheism? Where do you see these practical atheisms in your own life?
8. What do these things show us about our need for Jesus?

CHAPTER TEN

LEADERSHIP

"And the country had entered a time
when it was easier for a man . . .
to 'get big' than to save himself, if need be,
by getting smaller."[1]

I n his novel, *Jayber Crow*, Wendell Berry portrays two farmers and one plot of land. The two farmers are father-in-law and son-in-law. In time, the one plot of land will pass from the older to the younger. When Wendell writes about this farm, I think about congregations, communities, and nations. When Wendell describes these two farmers, I think about two differing ways to lead congregations and communities, organizations and families—one wise and the other, not so much.

In the hands of the older farmer, the long fruitfulness of the farm, with its creatures, soils, trees, fields, and workers rises from a leadership style which values patience, longevity, dignity, the limits of creatures, local knowledge, and a resistance to using more than what one needs. In contrast, the other farmer has no patience for this way of things, and no sense to respect the one who would graciously teach him if allowed. In contrast to the older farmer, the other one "thought the farm existed to serve and enlarge him."[2] Over the years, as the older man fades and the other one asserts his will on the land and the

193

family, both unravel with misuse. The young farmer works "too fast and too rough." "He lacked sympathy and was too hard on things."[3] Field, worker, creature, and family suffer as the farm serves as the stool on which the hasty farmer props his boots and strives for his own greatness.

The kings of Israel were not immune to leading poorly. Patience, a capacity for waiting, resisting immediate gratification or exploitation so that land and people can rest; these views are hard to come by. Famously and tragically, the kingdom was divided when a king, Solomon's son, listened to the wrong advice. The people were tired. The old and the wise, who had served as Solomon's advisors, encouraged the king to recognize limits, to give the people a break, and to take, instead, a long view. Nurture the people and the people would follow him wholeheartedly. In contrast, other advisors urged the king to take a hard approach. They felt it imperative to ignore limits, to identify fatigue as excuse, and to demand more from them than they can give. The idea was to beat the people down and to exploit every ounce from them. Like Wendell's farm story, the kingdom splintered and weakened (1 Kings 12:1–24).

Jesus' own disciples were tempted to "lord" their leadership over people. Jesus had no interest in such leadership (Matt. 20:25). Jesus critiqued the leaders of his day. "They tie up heavy burdens, hard to bear, and lay them on people's shoulders, but they themselves are not willing to move them with their finger" (Matt. 23:4).

Here in Ecclesiastes 10, the Preacher also has two differing kinds of leaders on his mind. "There is an evil that I have seen under the sun," he says, "as it were an error proceeding from the ruler" (Eccl. 10:5). Stepping outside the church doors in Ecclesiastes 5 and from there having surveyed the series of evils that remain, the Preacher adds foolish leaders to his list. God does not remove foolish leaders from our lives. Nor does he give us immunity from becoming foolish in our leadership. Just because we follow God, this does not mean that we aren't capable of folly. Just because the Lord attends our ministry with fruitfulness does not mean that we ourselves are without error or its potential. The Westminster Confession of Faith recognizes this point, for example, when referring to the sacraments. The efficacy of baptism and the Lord's Supper does not "depend upon the piety or intention of him that does administer it."[4] Leaders make mistakes. Leaders sin. God doesn't quit.

When we are fortunate to experience wise leadership, it sets the tables of our lives with good food that is knowledgeably prepared, fairly portioned, and generously given. In contrast, folly in leadership breaks the table legs, dirties both floor and food, and makes a joke of it all. Any of us called to lead, whether as a king or governor, or as a parent, teacher, pastor, project manager, coach, or friend, will need the grace of the Preacher's wisdom. Those of us who follow, pray that our leaders can lay to heart the Preacher's words.

Erring leaders make it hard to discern the presence of God in our lots and lives, because erring leaders promote the wrong people, act as if they aren't human like the rest of us, and talk big. In doing so, the people they lead suffer.

PROMOTING THE WRONG PEOPLE

Once I grabbed a milk jug and poured its contents onto my cereal for breakfast. My first bite soured my mouth, cringed my face, and turned my stomach. I shot a look into my spoon and then threw a stare onto the milk jug. The jug was filled with buttermilk. I had grabbed the wrong jug! The thick white paste draped heavy over the brown flakes of bran and sat like sour chunks of curd in my mouth. When one of my people heard this tale, she squinted her eyes and pursed her lips and quick-shivered as if she had sucked a lemon and said, "My lands, I like buttermilk, but boy, I'd never imagine putting it on cereal!" Sometimes we put things where they weren't meant to be. The result is a sour taste and the threat of nausea.

The proverbs of the wise apply this idea of putting things where they were not meant to be, and this to our hurt, to putting fools in charge. "Like snow in summer or rain in harvest, so honor is not fitting for a fool" (Prov. 26:1). "Whoever sends a message by the hand of a fool cuts off his own feet and drinks violence" (Prov. 26:6). "Like an archer who wounds everyone is one who hires a passing fool or drunkard" (Prov. 26:10). People get hurt when folly is put in charge.

The Preacher now adds his proverbs to this theme. By doing so, he seems to answer the "why" question. "Why does it hurt people when folly gets promoted?" Because foolish leaders have their wires crossed. They exalt themselves and deem wise only those things which will do the same. Wisdom gets viewed as folly. The wise are overlooked and passed over.

The old farmer looked out over his farm. He took a long view of the work required of it and the rest needed for the work to last and said, "Wherever I look, I want to see more than I need." The other farmer saw opportunity to get big fast. He responded, " 'Whatever I see, I want. . . . Why . . . would a man plow just forty acres of a farm he could plow all of?' He would say these things leaning back in his chair."[5] He would say these things to devalue the old farmer all over town.

A male butterfly will pass by a living female of his own species in favor of a painted cardboard one, if the cardboard one is larger than himself and larger than her. While the living female butterfly opens and closes her wings in vain, her life and theirs together seem small. The male has eyes for larger things. He gives his time and attention to the cardboard.[6]

Folly leads us to overlook what is small and what would bless us in order to chase after what is large and what in the end will leave us barren. This is why foolish leaders hurt people. They overlook what they ought not in order to honor what they most want for themselves. For this reason, just like a bully who looks for someone who values his bullying to join him, so a foolish leader looks to promote those who value his folly. Overlooked, then, the wise.

FOOLS FLOCK TOGETHER

The Preacher puts this mix-up that hurts us front and center with an analogy that might bother us. He has already told us a few stories about those who gain access to leadership who shouldn't, and the leaders who should but go forgotten under the sun (Eccl. 4:13; 9:16–17). "Folly is set in many high places," he says, "and the rich sit in a low place. I have seen slaves on horses, and princes walking on the ground like slaves" (Eccl. 10:6–7).

Some of us are immediately offended by this poetry. We value the story of a slave who gains freedom and rises to nobility. We value the humility of the rich who sit in a low place. Our offense likely comes, however, from hearing these words in light of our own cultural uses of them rather than as Solomon understood them.

For example, sometimes the sages cast "the rich" into a negative light. "Better is a poor man who walks in his integrity than a rich man who is crooked in his ways" (Prov. 28:6). But at other times the sage uses the term "rich" to identify the faithful, fair, patient, and hard-working character of a person. "A slack hand causes poverty, but the hand of the diligent makes rich" (Prov. 10:4). "A faithful man will abound with blessings, but whoever hastens to be rich will not go unpunished" (Prov. 28:20). Notice that the Preacher does not contrast the rich "in a low place" with the "poor" but instead with folly "in many high places." The Preacher uses the word "rich" here, not to identify material possessions, but to identify the true, steady, and faithful character of a person from which a measure of wealth generally comes. "Rich" does not refer to the lottery winner or to the heir or the thief. "Rich" refers here to the one who worked long and hard, and from such work and faithfulness wealth came. The Preacher's point is that an erring leader overlooks this kind of faithful character and places impatient, wandering, slothful, get-rich-quick schemers tragically in charge. Like the young man on Wendell's farm, he does not understand what long-term health of the farm will require and possesses no interest in learning.

Similarly, "slave" in this analogy is contrasted not with workers or freed persons but with "princes." Again, the Preacher follows the sage tradition. "It is not fitting for a fool to live in luxury, much less for a slave to rule over princes" (Prov. 19:10). The Preacher doesn't refer here to black slaves and their horrendous mistreatment within the American historical narrative. In contrast, "slaves" as used by the Preacher would refer to criminals or debtors or prisoners of war. In 1 Kings 9:15, Solomon utilized war captives for work.[7] His poetry and his proverb state the general truth that it is normatively unwise to put criminals serving their sentence or debtors who cannot manage themselves or prisoners of war from a foreign land into positions of authority and care over people.

In addition, the Preacher's choice to use a proverb instead of prose to make this point matters. A proverb states something that is normative not final. Joseph after all rises from slavery to lead Egypt. What the Preacher does is to apprentice us in human conversation with our neighbors. Everyone we do life with will have stories of bosses, parents, leaders, coaches, and politicians with whom they have experienced the blessings and the trials of following. We ourselves will have stories of our own folly. We needn't pretend otherwise or refuse to recognize this fact with our neighbors.

A good leader is hard to find and is often found in unexpected places, like a stable or a carpenter's shop, or on a cross like a thief. Sometimes true wisdom looks nothing like those who possess power and position, but instead like a poor carpenter who loved his enemies and for which his enemies killed him. Sometimes the triumph celebrated reveals the folly honored. Sometimes the true king goes unnoticed by the foolish. Jesus came as the poor wise man that delivered the city. He is the prince who walks as a servant while lesser men ride in honor under the sun.

FOOLISH LEADERSHIP RESISTS ITS HUMANITY

Sometimes human beings who are given authority and power start to act as if they are no longer subject to the same limits as everyone else. Where I come from in Southern Indiana, we refer to this phenomenon as "gettin' too big for one's britches." Jesus stated the fact of this phenomenon plainly, and he directed those who followed him otherwise. "It shall not be so among you," he beckoned. "Whoever would be great among you must be your servant, and whoever would be first among you must be slave of all" (Mark 10:43–44). Why would Jesus teach this? Perhaps because as someone has observed, "When a place is a mess, someone who thinks he is better than God has been at work there."[8]

Part of the mess we create as kings, leaders, parents, or ministry leaders stems from using our position as a means to escape our ordinary life. We come to believe that we are not like other people. But being uniquely gifted or solely positioned does not mean that we are uniquely unlimited or solely immune.

Some leaders emphasize superstition and magic. On a Saturday, I was doing yard work. I lifted up a pile of leaves and was met by the tense eyes and coiled rope of a large snake. Just because I was meditating on my sermon for the next morning didn't mean that I did not have to check the

199

wood and leaf piles in summer like everybody else. The problem is that erring leaders no longer check. They send people into situations and require them to overlook the precautions that slow us down, reveal our vulnerabilities, and frustrate but protect us. After all, "God favors us," we think to ourselves, or, "I'm the one with the power," we surmise. "How could God put me in this position and not think that I am special?"

But the Preacher opposes this sentiment with a proverb: "He who digs a pit will fall into it, and a serpent will bite him who breaks through a wall" (Eccl. 10:8). Steep pits and those serpents that coil up behind Middle Eastern walls exist under the sun as a matter of fact, no matter who we are. The wise take such facts to heart and plan accordingly. The foolish leader, in contrast, pays no attention to the railing and requires that others do the same. Railings do not apply to him, and he will not tolerate anyone who implies that they do.

We who follow such leaders love the way they make us feel. They tell us that we do not have to work as others do, or endure the setbacks or accidents that lesser neighbors face. The leader is our rabbit's foot, our four-leafed clover. With him, luck abounds. The fearful like the sense of control from harm that such leaders pledge. The proud seize the opportunity to dismiss weakness and to pursue risk unchecked. The leader is like a magic incantation. With him, nothing bad will happen. He will keep us from all harm.

The Preacher then takes it further. He declares that when we work with our hands, we get calluses, no matter who we are. In contrast, erring leaders believe that they can quarry stones and not get hurt or split logs without danger (Eccl. 10:9). Like a man who used a chainsaw with no safety glasses is a one-eyed leader who thinks his blindness is someone else's fault. Like a man who slept with another man's wife is a foolish leader who is shocked to find that his wife has left and his kids no longer want to speak to him. The erring leader not only acts like a magician promising an end to bad luck, he also believes that we shouldn't have discomfort or consequences to our work. We needn't work like other people do and yet the same rewards can be ours. Pain-free living is ours. We can quarry stones without bruises, split logs without danger. Not only will unforeseen accidents not happen to us but neither will the hardships of daily labor. We are entitled to comfort.

I am not a gun shooter. Friends who do shoot guns took me to the range once. I learned from them how to use the "safety" on the gun and how not to point the barrel as I walked around. A loaded gun with the safety turned off and pointed wrongly isn't less dangerous if held in the hands of a leader, but the erring ruler thinks that this is the case. The foolish leader imagines two people mishandling a gun. The one gets hurt, but no harm will come to the leader or to those who follow him. The Preacher's point is that a wise gun owner will not turn the safety on and hold the barrel up in the first place. Personas are not wise, actions are. We love this kind of leader. This promise of entitlement to get more for less (on the backs of others who get less for more) feels good. We don't have to endure what other people do.

Immunity defined by boundaryless luck and an entitlement to painless work forges an impatience for limits and an exploitation of time. "If the iron is blunt, and one does not sharpen the edge," the Preacher observes, "he must use more strength, but wisdom helps one to succeed" (Eccl. 10:10). The fool believes that he has no time to sharpen his worn-out blade. He believes that rest exposes either weakness or loss. Fatigue in persons or instruments is not permitted. People and instruments are made for our use. We will use them and will not slow down because they are worn nor will we take the time necessary to nourish, daily tune up, or recover their strength. Every action must have a large consequence in order to make a grand difference as fast as possible. There is little wonder then that when Israel asked Solomon's son for a break, in order that they might have the strength to go long term with him, the young man answered:

> My little finger is thicker than my father's thighs. And now, whereas my father laid on you a heavy yoke, I will add to your yoke. My father disciplined you with whips, but I will discipline you with scorpions. (1 Kings 12:10–11)

He had no category for taking a long view by going slow, taking strategic rest, and spending a day doing nothing but attending to the humdrum and boring necessity of sharpening tools. Fools get bored with necessary and lasting things. They are entertained and dazzled by fly-by-night flashes of moment. But for all of their shortcuts, they double their work and forfeit stamina for depth and distance. Erring rulers are amateur sprinters running with shoes whose worn soles they find it a waste of time to patch. For that, they "must use more strength" than is actually necessary. They view "success" as impatiently doing large and flashy things now. They consume time and use people in order to achieve it. They know nothing of the dignity of people, tools, rest, work, and necessary virtue for the long haul.

We love these leaders because they offer us immediate gratification; they see boredom as waste, flash as value. Our tools and our neighbors are made for us to use in order to get what we want. Time serves our disinterest in mundane attention to long-term dignity. Success does the big and the notable and all right now. Tools and neighbors are steps for our feet. We climb upon them in order to bask in the glow. Tools and neighbors are disposable cameras. We use them to produce what we want and then throw them away.

When I played freshman football, I played quarterback. The coach put a red mesh jersey on me. This meant that while we scrimmaged, the defensive players were not allowed to hit me. But then, once a week, when the plays we called weren't for practice but for an actual game, my wearing a red mesh jersey was not allowed. Hitting me was fair and expected. It is as if the Preacher says to us that leadership isn't practice. The game is real. Leaders and followers under the sun are available to get hit. Choosing a life that enables us to indulge luck, entitlement, and immediate gratification through the frantic use of neighbors and tools hurts peoples and communities.

So, the Preacher adds a bit more poetry. "If the serpent bites before it is charmed, there is no advantage to the charmer" (Eccl. 10:11). What good is a leader who does not know how to wisely handle the threatening situation in front of him and believes that he requires no learning to counter the ignorance he currently possesses? Having such a leader is like having a snake charmer, who for all of his pomp and words, dazzle and show, still gets bitten by the rising cobra. There was no ultimate advantage to that generation, no matter how the one in charge dressed, danced, and chanted. The community got snake bit.

When a leader does enough crossword puzzles, he or she will have to sharpen the pencil like anyone else. Sometimes the things that happen to us result simply from the fact that we live under the sun. We get hurt splitting logs, not because God is against us or we didn't keep God happy or Satan kicked our ladders out from under us, but simply because this is the way life is in the fallen world under the sun, no matter who we are, leader or follower, saint or sinner.

Followers also have trouble here. Some come to believe that their leaders possess superhuman strength. Their leaders are saviors not servants. We expect them to dig without falling, to never get hurt, to never slow down for the sake of surrendering to and handling what limits them and us. Foolish followers find foolish leaders and love to have it that way. As long as our leaders are saviors we needn't look plainly at our vulnerabilities or our own needs for responsibility or change. In such seasons we constantly sift through churches or teachers or organizations, always looking for someone who will not require us to change but allow us to hold onto superstition, entitlement, and impatient uses of time, tools, and neighbors. Such leaders tell us that we needn't look at the world as it is and that we needn't feel what it actually means that we are without hope save in the Lord and his wisdom and mercy.

Politicians city Council
President Congress

FOOLISH LEADERS ARE
ALWAYS TALKING BIG

In John Bunyan's *The Pilgrim's Progress*, two travelers, named Christian and Faithful, come upon a neighbor. After chatting on and on, Faithful finally asks the neighbor a question. "What is the one thing that we shall at this time found our discourse upon?" The neighbor answers.

> What you will: I will talk of things Heavenly, or things Earthly; things Moral, or things Evangelical; things Sacred, or things Prophane; things past, or things to come; things foreign, or things at home; things more essential, or things circumstantial; provided that all be done to our Profit.[9]

Eventually finding himself worn out by this neighbor's words, Faithful expresses his fatigue to Christian and asks who this neighbor is. Christian responds, "His name is *Talkative* . . . from *Prating-Row*; and notwithstanding his fine tongue, he is but a sorry fellow." Faithful is surprised at Christian, for the neighbor named Talkative "seems to be a very pretty man." Christian answers that to a stranger this neighbor seems pretty, but to those back home who know Talkative, he is like "the work of a Painter, whose pictures show best at a distance; but very near, more unpleasing." Faithful asks for further explanation, and as Christian describes one who is all talk but no substance he says of Talkative: "This man is for any company, and for any talk . . . all he hath lieth in his tongue."[10]

According to the Preacher, an erring leader "multiplies words" (Eccl. 10:14). In fact, when in this condition we love to hear ourselves talk, we are consumed with our own thoughts and words, giving full attention to what we ourselves want to say. "The lips of a fool consume him" (Eccl. 10:12). Always talking from beginning to end, he or she dominates the conversation but all with no actual knowledge or willingness to learn (Eccl. 10:13). Anxious to preserve high opinions of themselves or proud to demonstrate their superiority, erring leaders are big talkers. Exaggeration and promise on the basis of arrogance without information, the erring leader requires others to believe that he knows certainly what will happen with such and so plan. Fools promise that everything will be fixed because they know everything that will happen.

We followers love how it feels when a person makes mysteries certain, the future figured out, and the unknown plain as day. The problem is that no human being can actually do this. Parents, pastors, coaches, and politicians want to secure every possible good future for those they serve. But wisdom admits that we live each day with more that is unknown than known. In the quiet, the wise ponder the unknown by prayerfully taking stock of the known we possess, however small. In contrast, "a fool multiplies words, though no man knows what is to be, and who can tell him what will be after him?" (Eccl. 10:14).

Meanwhile, the fool uses words to disguise his lack of knowledge. Always pretending that he knows more than he does, he cannot humble himself to ask others to teach him things. The constant pretension to need no one to teach him, coupled with the unending swirl of words to secure allegiances and autographs and constituencies, "wearies" the fool "for he does not know the way to the city" (Eccl. 10:15). That is, while he pontificates mysteries that he can't possibly know, he ignores learning what any human being needs to know in order to navigate each ordinary day. He promises the moon but won't stop and ask for directions. He climbs the pulpit but won't wash a dish.

An old fable captures this picture of a leader who will not admit his need to ask a question and the impact of a people who follow such a leader. In Hans Christian Anderson's *The Emperor's New Suit*, an emperor loves clothes and agrees to buy a new suit. Those selling the suit set up looms and get hard at work on nothing but air. They then clothe the emperor with air. The emperor, thinking himself stupid if he admits that he cannot see the suit, gladly pays the money owed to those who made it for him. The emperor's followers also pretend to see the suit, afraid to admit what they cannot see when asked by the emperor how it looks. So the emperor preens down the street wearing nothing but a suit made of air as all the people cheer and laud the embarrassing sight with all honor. No one can see the suit, but no one will admit it. Finally, a child calls out and declares that he cannot see the new suit.

Some of us love this kind of leadership. The future is on our leader's shoulders. He will fix whatever comes and can explain whatever we can't. He never has anything to learn. Therefore, neither do we. What he says goes. His loneliness and practical ignorance don't matter to us. As long as he tells us about tomorrow, we can make it another day. Our ignorance is his bliss. His ignorance, we don't believe exists. If we did, we would leave him to find another Talkative upon whom we could gladly rest our futures.

The Preacher calls all of this "an evil" for our lament under the sun (Eccl. 10:5). Like the child among the crowds, the Preacher looks at the suitless emperor and points out that what gets celebrated as fashion is nothing but hot air posing as style.

The Preacher turns now and takes up a prophetic tone. "Woe to you!" he says (Eccl. 10:16). A generation experiences heartache, sorrow, trouble, and distress when those who lead use the people's resources to indulge themselves. Such leaders seize the opportunity to "feast in the morning!" (Eccl. 10:16). Such feasting is not "at the proper time" and is used not to strengthen the wisdom and care of the land but instead to inebriate those in charge (Eccl. 10:17).

We love to follow those who do not distinguish time into "appropriate" and "inappropriate." When every moment is useful to please ourselves and when every resource is for our consumption, life is offered to us as free and for the taking. Individualism has marvelous perks until we imagine a house burned to the ground as firemen lie passed out from their lunchtime booze fest. We become like a pilot who crashed his plane. After several rounds of midafternoon cocktails, he ditched his responsibility to others and in the process ditched everyone's lives as well.

THE LEADERSHIP OF JESUS

In error, we promote sparkling fools and despise enduring character. In wisdom, Jesus disrobes and washes feet (John 13:5). He promotes the humble and opposes the proud.

In error, we use leadership as a means for giving us lucky immunity from consequence and accident. In wisdom, "when the days drew near for him to be taken up, [Jesus] set his face to go to Jerusalem" (Luke 9:51).

In error, we seek entitlement and demand that great reward come with painless effort. In wisdom, Jesus "came not to be served but to serve, and to give his life as a ransom for many" (Mark 10:45).

207

In error, we resist limits, wearing down neighbors and tools for our own gain. In wisdom Jesus, "wearied as he was from his journey, was sitting down beside the well" (John 4:6).

In error, we talk big about things we can't know while refusing to learn the ordinary things we need to know. In wisdom, because Jesus himself "has suffered when tempted, he is able to help those who are being tempted" (Heb. 2:18). "He learned obedience through what he suffered" (Heb. 5:8).

In error, we use time and resources inappropriately for our own lusts. In wisdom, Jesus said to those who overlooked him, "My time has not yet come, but your time is always here" (John 7:6).

What the Preacher laments, the One greater than he takes up. Jesus takes up every foolish leader that we have endured and every foolish act of leadership that we have perpetrated on others. Every act of Jesus promoting the humble, resisting entitlement, surrendering to limits, talking truly, and using time appropriately is applied to pay for our every act of indulging the proud, seeking immunity, demanding entitlement, exploiting limits, talking big, and using time inappropriately toward the hurt of others.

In his life, death, and resurrection Jesus recovers the character of God's leadership that Eden experienced. There, God led us in wisdom. Here, God will lead us still, wisely, until he comes and no more will he suffer a fool to reign.

QUESTIONS FOR DISCUSSION

1. What about this chapter sticks out to you?
2. Going to church doesn't mean that we won't have to deal with poor leadership in others or ourselves. What does this fact teach you about how God is doing things?

3. Choose one of the qualities of poor leadership—promoting the wrong people, seeking entitlements, creating a clique, talking big, resisting limits, misusing resources. Describe a time in which you had to endure this from another or in which you imposed it on another.

4. How do we come to terms with the Preacher's poetry and the word *slaves*?

5. How does our hassle with leadership under the sun point us to hope in Jesus?

209

RECOVERING OUR PURPOSE

Maybe that's why a broken machine always makes me a little sad, because it isn't able to do what it was meant to do. . . . Maybe it's the same with people. If you lose your purpose . . . it's like you're broken.[1]

M y kids and I stood near South Conner Avenue in Joplin, Missouri. Along with thousands of others, we came to provide help to a community recovering from one of the worst tornados in American history. The scenes overwhelmed the senses. Death was everywhere. The city looked like a set of buildings that an eight-year-old made out of Legos. A bully came through and kicked through these Lego buildings as if they were his kickball. He laughed and offered no regard—or was it a tantrum of anger, a destructive bout from despair? Whichever, the bully kicked the hospital as well as the parking lot, the high school as well as the shed. The wood, metal, and bone were scattered about into miles of disconnected pieces. Neighbors bled and wept.

The nihilist has his suspicions confirmed. God is dead and so are we.

The cynic hands out fliers and makes speeches on the illusion of material gain.

The opportunist sells water bottles at inflated prices.

The hedonist has sex . . . again.

The Christian escapist holds up signs pronouncing God's judgment upon the city.

But most neighbors, regardless of their beliefs, react as if a tornado ripping out the teeth from life's gums is wrong. In fact, most neighbors respond as if neighbor help describes the most natural thing we could do. In this setting, God gets cursed or worshipped again. Either way, the community cannot ignore him. It is as if everyone recovers hints of memory and relates with a residue of Eden. Neighbor love shows up in a local place in the presence of God and everyone—whether angry or weeping—acts as if evil exists and recovers a profound sense that we were made for something infinitely better than this.

In Joplin, the tornado burgled the letters *J*, *l*, *i*, and *n* from the Joplin High School sign. The wind-looted sign simply read, "op High School." Someone from the wreckage added two letters, *H* and *e*. Surrounded by debris and ruin, the sign now read, "Hope High School."

The Preacher has used his entire message to make us stand as it were on Conner Avenue. He has wanted us to open our eyes and to look without blinders at the delights and distresses that we and our neighbors must actually endure under this sun. He wants us to come out of denial, to resist trite and simplistic responses to the horrific wreckage of once-Eden, so that we can, without naiveté, simpleism, folly, cruelty, or sentimentalism, add an *h* and an *e* to our lives and to those of our neighbors under the sun. He wants us to learn as human beings who follow God to engage what it means to "hate life" and to experience the meaninglessness of life that exists here in Eden lost.

But the Preacher is no nihilist. He is no cynic. He is neither a hedonist nor a religious escapist. Human purpose is not lost. God is not dead. Death comes for us all, but it cannot destroy ordinary joys empowered by God among the goodness of things that refuse to quit. And here, to conclude the book, from within the desecrated remains of God's creation, the Preacher looks at it all square in its ugly face and earnestly declares: "The end of the matter; all has been heard. Fear God and keep his commandments, for this is the whole duty of man" (Eccl. 12:13).

A court hears all the testimony regarding a particular matter. Each voice that has some bearing toward rightly discerning the facts, speaks. The judge listens. With testimonies, circumstances, and facts sprawled out like papers out of order on a table, the judge takes up each paper, locates where it goes, recollects order to the pages, and then renders a verdict. "All has been heard." The matter has come to its end. The time has come. We must draw our conclusions. The Preacher has let us hear the voices of human experience under the sun. Now the end of his message has come. What is the conclusion we are meant to draw from this? Powerfully, that our vain lives retain a God-saturated purpose. God has the last word and his word is good. Believing and following this God describes our "whole duty" or purpose in life. God is our purpose.

WE ARE PURPOSED TO FEAR GOD

When I think of the word *fear*, I unfortunately think of *Night of the Living Dead*. I was five years old and supposed to lie sleeping in the back seat of my young parents' car in what we refer to nowadays as "an old drive-in." While my parents watched this horror movie, so did I! I can still see the scenes in my mind of zombies coming through woods and eating people. Terror and horror resulted.

When the wise man uses the word *fear*, he does not have *Night of the Living Dead* in mind. He's not saying to us, "Be horrified about God, for God is like a zombie who is going to pull you like a frog off a tree and eat you raw." The Preacher does not have "slavish fear" in mind.[2] We do not respond to God as if God were a monster who seeks to destroy everything good about our lives. He is not like a criminal whom we must blackmail in order to keep ourselves and our families safe from harm. God is no spook in the night. He is not an abusive husband around whom we and the children must walk on eggshells, or else. Some thirty-six times, the Preacher has spoken of God in this book of his, and he has not described God as a character of horror from which we must hide.

To fear God is set in contrast to the one who enters God's house spouting off dreams and big promises, and these with no follow-through. Garnering attention and securing praise from others for the purpose of oneself misses the point and demonstrates a misplaced regard. "For when dreams increase and words grow many, there is vanity; but God is the one you must fear" (Eccl. 5:7). Likewise, here in Ecclesiastes 12, fearing God puts God front and center of our lives. The Preacher has made this governing regard for God amid the vanities under the sun plain. We look to our lot as God's gift. We discern through our disquiets and delights, his presence. We see him making his purposes stand amid the mystery of the seasons of our lives under the sun. He alone can make straight what is crooked. Whenever we encounter what is not known or is unexplainable, we recognize that God possesses the knowledge of it. When we are uncertain regarding which good road to try, we do so believing that, either way, "the one who fears God shall come out from both of them" (Eccl. 7:18). No matter how neighbors oppress each other or misuse one another, we maintain that God is our Creator and that he created us with dignity (Eccl. 7:29). Our days and deeds are in his hands (Eccl. 9:1). Death will not have the last word. Our spirits return to God. Everything wrong will be made right and every right thing will find commendation. God has spoken in the world. Amid all the voices of the nihilist, the cynic, the opportunist, the hedonist, and the escapist, this speech from God we know as his commands. These form the worldview we love, the way of thought by which we seek to live our lives. To fear God, in other words, recognizes that all of this life under the sun has its end in him and so do we. The one who does not fear God looks to other commands, other explanations, and other responses to the lots, seasons, circumstances, and uses of our lives under the sun. This one has an outlook and way of interpreting life under the sun as "wicked." "He does not fear before God" (Eccl. 8:13). Such persons turn somewhere other than to God for gain, purpose, explanation, and wisdom in the world.

LOCATING SOUND WORDS

Imagine a family caught within a battle. Their home is war weary. They must flee from it in order to find against all hope a refuge or shelter. Along the way, the bombs fall. Armies with guns ravage their streets and shops. The family gets separated. Two young kids, brother and sister, flee into the woods. For over a year, they hide out in local forests and makeshift sleeping places, living on scraps of food. They see and hear horrid things. Injustice, oppression, tears, greed, and neighbor hatred abound. Years later, as adults, they tell their story. Someone asks them how it was that they kept sane and retained their belief in beauty when they were berated with so much misuse, betrayal, oppression, and death. One of them pulls out a faded and torn letter from his pocket. "These words," he says. "Every night we would reread this letter with Father's handwriting. Just before the bombs fell it was my birthday. Our mother and father had written down for us their thanksgivings and their wishes for us in our lives. Separated and savaged, we could easily lose ourselves. But somehow seeing the handwriting and locating those words reminded us of where we came from and what our futures were and to whom we once belonged and to whom we belonged still, despite it all."

The Preacher now tells us something like this. "Of making many books there is no end." The opinions, ways, histories, and actions of people under the sun confront us with many diverse ideas, tragedies, and explanations regarding life and God, along with multiple and conflicting purposes for the way life should be. "Much study is a weariness of the flesh" (Eccl. 12:12). Sometimes the sheer number of conflicting voices causes us to quit on the idea that anything true exists, or that if it does, we can find it. But the Preacher maintains that within all of the voices swirling under the sun, the "one Shepherd," the voice of the Lord,[3] remains present and active, giving us "the words of the wise." These Shepherd-given wisdom words are "collected sayings." Like a letter from home daily reminding us of whose we are and what remains true while the war rages round us, these "are like goads, and like nails firmly fixed" (Eccl. 12:11). A goad is a long stick that guides cattle or oxen and keeps them from wandering off the way. Loosely fit nails edge and rise out of place with each passing day of wear and use of its floors. These must constantly feel the weight of a hammer pushing them back down. Firmly fixed nails hold as the weight of the world presses in on its joints and beams. "The collected sayings" that "are given by one Shepherd" and the commandments of God are set before us together as one. God's words are central to our whole vocation in life as human beings.

So the Preacher oriented his days around searching out these words, giving his days to "weighing and studying and arranging" these "many proverbs with great care." He arranged his life around the pursuit of "words of delight." Out of this pursuit "the preacher also taught the people knowledge" and "uprightly he wrote words of truth" (Eccl. 12:9–10).

King Solomon "spoke 3,000 proverbs, and his songs were 1,005."

He spoke of trees, from the cedar that is in Lebanon to the hyssop that grows out of the wall. He spoke also of beasts, and of birds, and of reptiles, and of fish. And people of all nations came to hear the wisdom of Solomon, and from all the kings of the earth, who had heard of his wisdom. (1 Kings 4:32–34)

Amid the swirl of voices under the sun, the Shepherd's words, the commands of God, shed light on everything in creation and providence. The Shepherd knows, not just the names of the sheep and the words those sheep need, in contrast to the voice of strangers, in order for them to find green pastures, but the Shepherd also wisely reckons with the landscape and weather for his sheep. He is knowledgeable about God in contrast to the gods of the nations around him. But wisdom and vocation also cause him to learn about trees and grass and rain, along with the patterns of wolves, how to care for sick animals and birth lambs as a wise one rather than a fool. As we walk across this creaky attic of the world, we watch our step and learn which beams of creation, providence, and redemption are firmly fixed and which beams will give way and collapse beneath our feet, leaving us flat on our backs after we crash through to the room beneath us.

TEMPTED TO MOVE BEYOND

A paradox of vocation and purpose rises for our consideration at this point. An old saying from the monks regarding a wise man named Moses and his student captures it.

In Scetis, a brother went to Moses to ask for advice. He said to him, "Go and sit in your cell and your cell will teach you everything."[4]

The young man wanted to know what to do with his life. The wiser man answered by telling him to go back home and do what presents itself there. Grand purpose

217

wasn't found in moving beyond where he was. Purpose was found rather by remaining. Surrendering to a local life with ordinary days over a long period of time would discover everything he needed to know.

We come to the book of Ecclesiastes like this young brother seeking advice regarding what purpose toward which we should focus our ambitions. As we have read the book, it is as if the wise man asks us to sit with him for a moment. He'd like to tell us a story. So we sit there together in two rocking chairs on a porch that gives us a wide view of the hills and valleys of the place. The wise man begins to tell us about his life. We are surprised to learn that the story he has to tell us is his own. He too once searched to find out what grand purpose should suit him. In his search, he gave himself to considering and sometimes to experimenting with every voice and any idea under the sun. He tells us about the jokes he has told and heard, the alcohol he has drunk, the art he has loved, the nature that has enthralled him, the money he has spent, the material possessions he amassed, the music he danced to, the sex he has known with women, his ambitions and the applause of people that he has trusted, and the hard work he gave himself to in order to possess and experience all of these things.

Then, he begins to survey the many neighbors he has met and the many books he has studied. The conversations and the terrible plight of many people in the world cause him to pause. He seems frustrated. "People are full of dignity, but they shred it every day and misuse one another," he says. As his story continues, he turns pale and somber. "I am no different," he says. "I too do this." Then as we listen, we are shocked to hear him say he hated life. No amount of art, money, music, or sex could satisfy his soul or make the world a better place. He tells us then about his wrestling match with God and what it feels like at times to live with the unknown every day while God knows but does not act in the manner we want. He tells us about the mixed blessing the house of God is—sometimes the worst pains and the biggest foolery go on in there. And then suddenly, the wise man laughs. He laughs hard and long. He shakes his head and begins to talk to us about the surprising joy he has found and how strange it was to learn where to find it.

At this point, our ears perk up. "There is true joy in the world? And you know where to find it?" "Oh, yes," he says. "Yes I do, now." We ask advice about this part of his story. He pauses and then offers us a sort of parable. He says to us:

"I lost my pencil once. I searched the tabletop, inspected the floor beneath, rummaged through my backpack, and went fishing into my pockets. I stood up. I investigated the tables next to me. I bent down and peered into the nooks and crannies between them. I walked around, talked to everyone in the room, and finally asked a neighbor if he had a pencil that I could borrow.

" 'I seem to have lost mine,' I said.

"That neighbor smiled and chuckled. 'There's a pencil right there on your ear,' the neighbor said. 'Is that the one you lost?'

"Surprised, I reached my hand to my ear and there it was. I had set my pencil to rest there, as is my habit. Embarrassed, I too smiled and chuckled.

"Sometimes the things we go searching for are with us all along."

After a long pause he says to us. "You will be tempted to think that you must move beyond the wisdom words of God in order to make a difference and find your purpose, Ecclesiastes 12:12 says. His words will at times seem too small and quiet a thing amid the clamor and importance of the world. You will be tempted to think that you need something more than your relationship with God in order to prove worthy and credible under the sun. But I tell you, after everything is said and done, the end of the matter, the grand purpose for which we live, the 'whole duty' of your life is this: trust God, follow what he says, and this, right where you are. This was your purpose in Eden. Your purpose it remains. When your spirit returns to God it will forge your purpose still, for the rest of days."

"But how?" we ask.

THE SHEPHERD'S VOICE IN COMMUNITY

There on the porch, we remember that the question before us is "the whole duty of *man*" (Eccl. 12:13). Our "whole duty" is the same as our neighbor's. Each of us will differ in what our hearts find to do (Eccl. 11:9). But no matter who we are, God, his ways, where we are, and all for him, forms the human purpose. Likewise, the sayings of wisdom are "the words of the wise." These are teachings passed down by a community of the wise, collections from generation to generation, by those who went before us but who also gave their lives to this purpose of the one Shepherd. Moreover, this wisdom is taught to the people, not just to us individually, as we personally read this book (Eccl. 12:9).

Consequently, fulfilling our "whole duty" in life, and doing this wisely, disrupts our attempts to go it alone. "Woe to him who is alone when he falls and has not another to lift him up!" (Eccl. 4:10). "How can one keep warm alone?" (Eccl. 4:11). "Two are better than one. . . . A threefold cord is not quickly broken" (Eccl. 4:9, 12). In contrast, "Whoever isolates himself seeks his own desire; he breaks out against all sound judgment" (Prov. 18:1).

Those of us hurt by the dark sides of community are tempted to choose folly as a response. In arrogance we resist the counsel of Scripture that "two are better than one." We go it alone and declare that we need no one. But this response hurts us as much as the wound that we have no desire to repeat. We need grace to recognize the wheat from the weeds. Part of this grace identifies neighbors, given to us by God, who bring us news of the one Shepherd, amid the strife under the sun. For this reason, Jesus taught "us" to pray, *Our* Father, give *us*, forgive *us*, lead *us* not, and deliver *us* (Matt. 6:9–13).

When Christian fell beneath the waves, John Bunyan tells us, he was nearly swallowed up and lost altogether, were it not for the grace of his companion, named Hopeful.

> Christian began to sink, and crying out to his good friend, Hopeful, he said, I sink in deep Waters; the Billows go over my head, all the Waves go over me. Selah. Then said the other, Be of good cheer, my Brother, I feel the bottom, and it is good.[5]

THE SHEPHERD'S VOICE IN JUDGMENT

Part of our help to pursue our human purpose also comes when recognizing that all the secrets of this vain life, along with everything good and evil, will be brought to light, sorted out, and set right. Every neighbor will stand before God to be judged by his good character (Eccl. 12:14). In this life, the Preacher does not pretend with us. Justice under the sun is imperfect at best and often poorly rendered. "Because the sentence against an evil deed is not executed speedily, the heart of the children of man is fully set to do evil" (Eccl. 8:11).

The Preacher has named and grieved over the hypocrisies, oppressions, greedy schemes, injustices, and pains that even good people must encounter in and out of their seasons under the sun. In light of all of this damage, it can seem cruel that God has placed eternity into our hearts (Eccl. 3:11) unless, in spite of it all, eternity still remains relevant for us who, in season and out, must strive meaninglessly after wind through our disquiets and delights. The Preacher declares that eternity is relevant for the times and seasons in which we tend our lots. God is knowledgeable about our plight. He does not turn a blind eye, though it seems he has left the madness unattended. A day is coming in which God will step out from within the shadows and make himself plainly known. In that day, he alone will preach and every creature and thing and place will listen.

> I said in my heart, God will judge the righteous and the wicked, for there is a time for every matter and for every work. (Eccl. 3:17)

> For God will bring every deed into judgment, with every secret thing, whether good or evil. (Eccl. 12:14)

For many of us, judgment scares, threatens, and spooks us. But for the Preacher, judgment blesses us. For in it, a distinction will finally be made which lost Eden has refused to own. "The righteous" and "the wicked" and their ways within their seasons and times, will finally hear what was and is true about them. By this, the Preacher does not imply that the "righteous" are without sin and their own need of God. "Surely there is not a righteous man on earth who does good and never sins," he reminds us (Eccl. 7:20).

But King David, for all of his sins, differs still from King Ahab. Likewise, the disciples of Jesus, for all of their sins and misdeeds, still differ from the Pharisees who tried to kill Jesus. David was a man after God's own heart. Peter, James, John, and the others loved Jesus and gave their lives to glorify God through his grace. The sort of glory we sought and the life with God that we disregarded or clung to will be made known. Illusions flee. Pretensions evaporate. Secret evils are exposed, but so are secret goods. Noble moments and people rescued by grace but long overlooked and disregarded are hidden no more. God's judgment, the Preacher implies, not only condemns it also finally vindicates.

And so, the poor and wise youth forgotten by the world in Ecclesiastes 4, or the poor who are unjustly oppressed in Ecclesiastes 5, or the righteous people "to whom it happens according to the deeds of the wicked" in Ecclesiastes 8, or the poor wise man forgotten and despised in Ecclesiastes 9, these will all finally find fair and true treatment, vindicated fully, when God judges the times.

When we are sinned against, all of us hunger and thirst for a righteous judgment, whether we follow God or not. When we see another human being mistreated and misused in our communities or on the news, we feel outraged and inwardly agitated; as when we watch a crime show on television and the wicked get away with it amid a botched justice system. It is only when we are the ones committing sin or when we are receiving a lifestyle benefit from those who are that we resist and complain about accountability and judgment.

Our human longing for right judgment makes sense. Good judgment is authentic. It says what is true. We know that when good judgments are rendered, one sibling doesn't take the fall for what another sibling did. We know that the victim of a crime receives a public declaration that what happened to her was not right. Likewise, the bearers of the family secret, misused, abused, and shamed, are given aid when another finally breaks the secret, comes along, and says, "What was done to you was wrong." The misused, mistreated, and victimized are cared for when good judgments are made. The hypocrite is found out. The schemer is foiled. The public good is defended. The one who did well by grace, so long overlooked, is finally honored. The eternity pressing into our hearts, the eternity that Eden was made for, the eternity that life under the sun beats up, stomps upon, ridicules, and dishonors, will finally also behold its vindication. God himself will take his rightful place and we, as Eden intended, will again bow, fully satisfied, as his creatures.

THE SHEPHERD'S VOICE IN OUR VOICE

By the Preacher's manner of life and conversation, he apprentices us, not only by what he says, but also by how he goes about it. We learn from him how it is that one who fears God can converse with his or her neighbors amid the lots, seasons, true joys, gainless pleasures, wise sayings, and foolish traumas that attend us all. We take what we learned about entering the house of God and apply it to the way we enter the God-present lives of our neighbors and our times.

Wisdom makes us quicker to listen and slower to speak. "All has been *heard*" (Eccl. 12:13). We learn the grace to weigh, study, arrange, and find wise truth among the voices and circumstances of our localities and generations (Eccl. 12:9–10). We learn that waiting, meditating, patience, time, and a willingness to withhold judgment on appearance serve us better than hasty reactions based on unmeditated conclusions. We are each prone to view the data in front of us without having surrendered it to God. We are prone to bend our neighbor's voices to what we think they should say rather than what they actually do. Quick to control, we learn little how to hear, to sit, and to wait.

Further, we are apprenticed by the wisdom of grace, not only to meditate and listen but also to discern what we encounter within our hearts and out there in the world. By means of sifting and meditating, we seek to locate those words of truth that can act like nails firmly fixed for our life and purpose. Then, after meditating and sifting, we speak. The Preacher taught and wrote out of the fruit of his slow meditation and daily sifting. In short, the Preacher does not teach us a way of following God that enables us to dismiss or distance ourselves from our neighbors or their plight. On the contrary, he listens, gives voice to everything noble and ignoble under the sun, and then sorts it out, without trite answers, beneath the gaze of God. The fear of God does not lead us to escape the strivings and traumas of once-Eden. The fear of God empowers us to enter it and, with his wisdom, to live and to speak a wise life, in our lot, through the ebb and flow of our seasons until we return home to him. In this, an alternative way of life and neighbor love out of love for God in our given lot, gives testimony. This testimony offers remembrance to what we were created for in Eden. It likewise hallows a future. For what will heavenly citizens do with their heavenly lives? We will do then what the Preacher calls us to cultivate and to practice now—to enjoy God in our lots where we are out of fear for him, regard for his words, and embodiment of his wisdom with the community we inhabit.

You hear a crash in the living room. It is a vase. It might have been a vase you loved. You have four children. After you hear the crash, the shouts magnify. "Mom! Dad!" Four different voices run your way to tell you, "I didn't do it. No. He did it. She hit me!" So there you are, encountering what's given. All has to be heard. You weren't there when the vase crashed. You don't actually know how it all started. You are brought into a story that has already taken place. In order to make some sense of that, you have to slow down and listen. Hasty reaction will likely render the wrong verdict with an emotional reaction built on irrational logic. Yet even seeking to hear creates problems.

We are selective with data. We like to reduce complexity, to simplify it. Some of us like to reduce disquiets, because we want everything to be happy. Others of us reduce delights because we are more familiar with sadness and hardship. The Preacher embodies a way of hearing that allows *both* to remain. We are created to enter mystery and contradiction with the fear of God and let it sit. For us who like control, we'd rather the vase not be broken in the first place. We'd rather the kids not blame each other. We'd rather be able to know, exactly in the moment, who's telling the truth and who's not. But life under the sun is not this way. We don't want to meditate. So now what?

Not only are we selective with data; when it comes to hearing, we are also noisy. We tend only to want to hear our own voice. We struggle to allow another point of view. And because of that, we struggle to hear. But we are created to hear, even to hear voices that are dissonant from our own. Even when Solomon himself says, "I hate life," we are created to hear a man seeking God say that he hates life. What do we do with this kind of dissonance? We want to close our ears, but we are called to listen and discern the voice of the one Shepherd in the mix. But we don't want to interpret or discern. So now what?

Others of us are willing to enter the meaningless data and listen to the trauma, but we don't want ultimately to say anything about it. It's like a person who gives us a dollar to make change. We feel grateful to receive the dollar. But we do not want to do the math in order to return the change and sort out the coins. So, we just steal the dollar or we give it back. But we resist making something of it in light of what doing the math would reveal.

So, a search for God rages all around us. Data wait for meditation, discernment, and wise conclusions. Everyone's temptation however is to partially select data to prove their own point of view. Let's use September 11 as an example. One person looks at September 11 and says, "There is no God. September 11 proves it." "Why?" we ask. "Just look at the violence and the innocent murdered. Add to that the fact that the murdering was done in God's name. Some Christians even responded to their bloodied and widowed neighbors and said, 'You deserve it. God is punishing you!' Others are saying that God is pleased with those who crashed their planes and exploded so many of their neighbors. So," he continues, "all of these competing God voices exist. Then there are the thieves and plunderers who roamed the devastated roads and took advantage of a vulnerable humanity experiencing a scarcity of basic needs. Then, look at the human response. Backlash of violence targeted against Middle Easterners. There's no answer; there's no justice. This is all that's given. This is all that we have to listen to. The end of the matter is this: there is no God."

In contrast, another one listens. She too enters the lament—cries out at the injustices, hates the violence, loves her neighbors, seeks the grace to love even her enemies. In response to the same data, she suggests instead, "There is a God. Strangers risked their lives for one another. Firemen and women, policemen and women, sacrificed their own futures for the sake of other neighbors. Passengers on an airplane resisted their own fear and gave their lives to hinder the carnage from being worse. Cell phone calls revealed statements of love, cherishing, remembering, forgiving, and blessing one another. Doctors and nurses rushed and took upon themselves the blood of strangers, in the blackout, in the ash, to comfort, to heal, to mend. Tribunals formed because somehow, inwardly, people long for judgment—for victims to have vindication, for us to declare to the world this way of treating God and neighbor is not right. Materialistic people give away money for strangers. Artists sing, paint, and write poems to remember and honor their neighbors. Places of worship are packed. They offer room for lament, for neighbors to ask the question, 'Why?' This sounds like instincts from Eden. After all has been heard," she concludes, "there is a God."

I spoke to a man once in the house of God. The day before, the doctor told the man that cancer was invading his body. Death was on his mind and announcing its soon arrival in his bones. That morning in church, a child, who had no knowledge of the terrible news, walked up to the man and gave him a gift. It was a flower.

"After all has been heard on the matter, what do you conclude?" The Preacher apprentices us to enter the questions, to hear, to honor, to discern, and to humbly and wisely answer. "Fear God," he concludes (Eccl. 12:13). For this pursuit identifies the grand purpose for which we were created in Eden and which remains for us still, even here in Eden lost.

THE SHEPHERD HIMSELF

Imagine a young boy or a girl whose father died years ago. An old friend of the child's father comes to town. He and the teen spend a day together. The teen hears stories about his dad and experiences hints of his dad's life and personality. That night, the mother asks, "Did you enjoy this day?" "Yes and no," the teen responds. "What do you mean?" the mother inquires. "Well," says the teen, "it was great to see Dad's friend. It almost felt at times like I could see Dad in the words of his old friend. That meant a lot." "But there's something still bothering you?" the mother replies. "Yes," says the teen. "It's still not the same as seeing Dad himself."

Perhaps if someone asks us whether we have enjoyed reading Ecclesiastes, we might similarly respond, "yes and no." We are grateful for the Preacher's message. He has shown us a great deal of wisdom that reveals to us true resemblances to how God relates to us under the sun. In the Preacher, we gain access to a wisdom apprenticeship for conversing with our neighbors and interpreting our lives in the fear of God. But the Preacher isn't God. In fact, the Preacher, or his namesake, Solomon, did not live up to the wisdom he had learned and taught. "Solomon did what was evil in the sight of the LORD and did not wholly follow the LORD, as David his father had done" (1 Kings 11:6). With this, we are invited to consider one last truth in this vain life under the sun. Every human wise man has fallen short of his own true wisdom. The Preacher cannot save the oppressed and the oppressor whose plight he has so deftly and humanly entered. The Preacher cannot save himself. Knowing wisdom and avoiding folly has no power in itself to rescue us. Like a fireman who saved someone from a burning building once but still struggles to relate without damaging family and friends by his temper, even wise teachers such as Abraham, Moses, David, Solomon, Peter, and Paul can do no more than amass an incomplete measure of wisdom in their lives. In them, we see glimpses of God. But they are not God for us.

So, "to read Ecclesiastes is to hear our Shepherd's voice."[6] We look through the human wise man that the Shepherd inspired for our help and on to the Shepherd himself for our hope and purpose. We thank the Preacher for mentioning the Shepherd in this way and at this time—an unusual term for a sage to use. For in it, God can remind us of what he showed Solomon's dad.

As we look out at the wants, the pastures, the paths, the deadness of soul, the valleys of death's shadow, and the presence of enemies, we engage these realities under the sun by contemplating God as our Shepherd. This Shepherd is the Lord, the want provider, the rest giver, the pasture and path leader, and the soul restorer. He is the valley walker, the "with me" overcomer, the comforter, the table preparer, the head anointer, the cup filler, the goodness and mercy sender, the house dweller, and the forever, all the days of my life, securer (Ps. 23).

Surveying under the sun and seeing once-Eden littered with shepherds who cannot or will not tend us amid its stark realities, God says that he himself will shepherd us. On a day of clouds and thick darkness under the sun, God will seek out those who have been scattered, go to any place to rescue us, to gather us home, to feed those of us who are hungry, to lead us, to give rest to the weary, to seek those of us who are lost, to mend those who are injured, to give strength to the weak, and to fight off and protect us from those who threaten to devour us (Ezek. 34:11–16).

Then God makes good on this promise. Jesus, the Son of David, the King, he comes into the wreckage under the sun. He is the Good Shepherd who knows his sheep by name. He will lay down his life for them, here in this vain world (John 10:1–18). The one Shepherd, the one greater than Solomon, he has come. The memory of Eden recovers. The promise of heaven awaits.

QUESTIONS FOR DISCUSSION

1. Talk about the Joplin story that begins this chapter. Describe how the Preacher's approach differs from the cynic, the opportunist, the hedonist, and the Christian escapist. What does this different approach teach us about how God approaches us in Joplin-like situations?
2. What does it mean to "fear God"? What does it not mean? How does this surprise you, inform you, or encourage you?
3. Sometimes the things we go looking for are with us all along. What do you make of this statement?
4. How do we discern the voice of the Lord under the sun? What role do community, judgment, and our own voices play in this discernment?
5. What is the purpose of our lives?
6. Describe the true Shepherd? What thanks and praise does he arouse in you?
7. As you look back over this book, summarize something of what it has been teaching you about God, the gospel in Jesus, your neighbors, the place in which you live, and your own life. How is it changing the way you relate to God, your neighbors, and the place in which you live?

NOTES

CHAPTER ONE: AN UNEXPECTED VOICE

1. Mike Carson, "The Keeper's Voice," in *The Keeper's Voice* (Baton Rouge, LA: Louisiana State University Press, 2010), 71.
2. C. S. Lewis, *A Grief Observed* (London: Faber and Faber, 1961), 29.
3. Ibid., 23.
4. Ibid., 7.
5. John Calvin, *Institutes of the Christian Religion*, ed. John T. McNeill, trans. Ford Lewis Battles, The Library of Christian Classics (Philadelphia: Westminster Press, 1960), 1.1.1–2.
6. Ibid., 1.1.1.
7. Philip Graham Ryken, *Ecclesiastes: Why Everything Matters* (Wheaton, IL: Crossway, 2010), 16.
8. Ibid.
9. J. I. Packer, *Knowing God* (Downers Grove, IL: InterVarsity, 1993), 104.
10. Some respected commentators suggest that this disparity exists because we are not meant to listen to the voice of Ecclesiastes as someone to imitate or follow. I do not follow this line of thinking. But I recommend an excellent commentary to understand this approach. See Tremper Longman, *The Book of Ecclesiastes*, The New International Commentary on the Old Testament (Grand Rapids: Eerdmans, 1998).
11. Quoted in John Stott, *Between Two Worlds: The Art of Preaching in the 20th Century* (Grand Rapids: Eerdmans, 1982), 30.
12. See Zack Eswine, "Sage Preaching for Postmodern Contexts," *Reformation & Revival Journal* 14 (2005).
13. Edward M. Curtis and John J. Brugaletta, *Discovering the Way of Wisdom: Spirituality in the Wisdom Literature* (Grand Rapids: Kregel, 2004), 192.
14. Zack Eswine, *Preaching to a Post-Everything World: Crafting Biblical Sermons That Connect with Our Culture* (Grand Rapids: Baker, 2008), 150.
15. Curtis and Brugaletta, *Discovering the Way of Wisdom*, 202.
16. Ibid., 194.

17 William P. Brown, *Ecclesiastes* (Louisville, KY: John Knox, 2000), 11–12.

18 Sidney Greidanus, *Preaching Christ from Ecclesiastes: Foundations for Expository Sermons* (Grand Rapids: Eerdmans, 2010), 4.

19 Michael A. Eaton, *Ecclesiastes*, Tyndale Old Testament Commentary (Downers Grove, IL: InterVarsity, 2009), 50.

20 Francis Schaeffer, *Death in the City* (Wheaton, IL: Crossway, 2002), 105.

21 Greidanus, *Preaching Christ from Ecclesiastes*, 4.

22 Eaton, *Ecclesiastes*, 53.

23 Curtis and Brugaletta, *Discovering the Way of Wisdom*, 199.

24 Packer, *Knowing God*, 104.

25 Lewis, *A Grief Observed*, 8.

26 Ibid., 9.

27 Ibid., 58.

CHAPTER TWO: AN UNEXPECTED METHOD

1 Robert Hass, "Iowa January," in *The Apple Trees at Olema: New and Selected Poems* (New York: HarperCollins, 2010), 265.

2 If one assumes Solomonic authorship.

3 Eccl. 1:13, 16, 17; 2:1, 15; 3:17–18; 8:16.

4 See Eccl. 1:3; 2:11; 3:9; 5:16.

5 Helen Lemmel, "Turn Your Eyes upon Jesus," *Glad Songs* (British National Sunday School Union, 1922).

CHAPTER THREE: FINDING GAIN

1 Robert Frost, "A Line-Storm Song," in *Everyman's Library*, ed. John Hollander (New York: Alfred A. Knopf, 1997), 47.

2 John Denver, "Sunshine on My Shoulders," *Poems, Prayers & Promises* (1971).

3 Mick Jones, "I Want to Know What Love Is," *Agent Provocateur* (Atlantic, November 5, 1984).

CHAPTER FOUR: HANDLING OUR PLEASURES

1 Augustine, "Homilies on the Psalms," in *Augustine of Hippo: Selected Writings*, trans. Mary T. Clark, The Classics of Western Spirituality (Mahwah, NJ: Paulist Press, 1984), 233.

2 Peter Kreeft, *Three Philosophies of Life* (San Francisco, CA: Ignatius Press, 1989), 15.

3 Joshua Wolf Shenk, *Lincoln's Melancholy: How Depression Challenged a President and Fueled His Greatness* (New York: Houghton Mifflin, 2005), 116.

4   Benedict, *The Rule of Saint Benedict* (New York: Penguin Classics, 2008), 21.

5   George Herbert, "The Temple," in *George Herbert: The Complete English Works* (New York: Alfred A. Knopf, 1995), 9–10.

6   Kerry Cohen, *Loose Girl: A Memoir of Promiscuity* (New York: Hyperion, 2008). Quoted in https://www.kirkusreviews.com/book -reviews/kerry-cohen/loose-girl/#review (accessed October 1, 2012).

7   Wallace Stevens, "Adagia," in *Opus Posthumus: Poems, Plays, Prose* (New York: Vintage, 1990).

8   Mark Goulston, "Why Are Americans So Unhappy?," http://www .huffingtonpost.com/mark-goulston-md/why-are-americans-so -unha_b_1112384.html (accessed November 25, 2011).

9   C. S. Lewis, *The Weight of Glory and Other Addresses* (New York: HarperCollins, 2001), 26.

CHAPTER FIVE: HATING LIFE AND BEING WISE

1   Nicolas Wolterstorff, *Lament for a Son* (Grand Rapids: Eerdmans, 1987).

2   J. R. R. Tolkien, *The Fellowship of the Ring* (Boston: Houghton Mifflin, 1987), 167.

3   John Calvin, *Institutes of the Christian Religion*, ed. John T. McNeill, trans. Ford Lewis Battles, The Library of Christian Classics (Philadelphia: Westminster Press, 1960), 1.1.1.

4   Westminster Larger Catechism, Question 28.

5   Cormac McCarthy, *The Stonemason: A Play in Five Acts* (New York: Vintage, 1998). Found at http://www.goodreads.com/quotes/50924 -the-rain-falls-upon-the-just-and-also-on-the (accessed February 13, 2013).

CHAPTER SIX: DEATH AND THE JOY OF AN ORDINARY LIFE

1   Thomas Gray, "Elegy Written in a Country Church Yard," http:// www.poets.org/viewmedia.php/prmMID/19371 (accessed December 15, 2011).

2   Jennifer Michael Hecht, *Doubt: A History* (New York: HarperSanFrancisco, 2004), 32.

3   Oscar Wilde, *The Picture of Dorian Gray* (New York: Modern Library, 1992), 145.

4   Flannery O'Connor, "A Good Man Is Hard to Find," in *The Complete Stories* (New York: Farrar, Straus and Giroux, 1971), 132.

5   For more on escapism or "simpleism" see Zack Eswine, *Preaching to a Post-Everything World: Crafting Biblical Sermons That Connect with Our Culture* (Grand Rapids: Baker, 2008), chaps. 2 and 4.

6   Brother Lawrence, *The Practice of the Presence of God* (New Kensington, PA: Whitaker House, 1982), 16, 24.

7   John Calvin, *Institutes of the Christian Religion*, trans. Henry Beveridge, 2 vols. (Edinburgh: Calvin Translation Society, 1845), 2:492.

8   Corrie Ten Boom, *The Hiding Place* (Grand Rapids: Chosen, 1971), 91.

9   Francis Schaeffer, *Letters of Francis A. Schaeffer: Spiritual Reality in the Personal Christian Life* (Wheaton, IL: Crossway, 1985), 82.

10 *The Shawshank Redemption* (Castlerock Entertainment, 1994).

CHAPTER SEVEN: KNOWING THE TIMES

1   Mary Austin, *The Land of Little Rain* (Carlisle, MA: Applewood, 2000), 6.

2   Wendell Berry, *A Continuous Harmony: Essays Cultural and Agricultural* (Washington, DC: Shoemaker & Hoard, 1972), 48.

3   Fernando Savatar, *The Questions of Life: An Invitation to Philosophy* (Malden, MA: Blackwell Publishers, 2002), 163.

4   "Beautiful" here is not an aesthetic judgment. Many of the events listed in Eccl. 3, such as war and death, are not beautiful in that sense. In fact, Michael V. Fox has argued that the Hebrew word should be translated as "fitting" rather than "beautiful" (*A Time to Tear Down and a Time to Build Up: A Re-Reading of Ecclesiastes* [Grand Rapids: Eerdmans, 2009], 209).

5   Tremper Longman, *The Book of Ecclesiastes*, The New International Commentary on the Old Testament (Grand Rapids: Eerdmans, 1998), 114.

6   Ibid., 115.

7   Benedicta Ward, *The Desert Fathers: Sayings of the Early Christian Monks* (New York: Penguin Classics, 2003), 60.

8   Charles Bridges, *Ecclesiastes* (Edinburgh: The Banner of Truth, 1960), 8.

9   Michael A. Eaton, *Ecclesiastes*, Tyndale Old Testament Commentary (Downers Grove, IL: InterVarsity, 2009), 159.

CHAPTER EIGHT: CHURCH, UNDER THE SUN

1   Philip Larkin, "Church Going," in *The Less Deceived* (Hessle, East Yorkshire: The Marvel Press, 1955).

2   Robert Faggen, ed., *Striving Towards Being: The Letters of Thomas Merton and Czeslaw Milosz* (New York: Farrar, Straus & Giroux, 1997), 162.

3   Larken, "Church Going."

4   William Lobdell, *Losing My Religion: How I Lost My Faith Reporting on Religion in America—and Found Unexpected Peace* (New York: HarperCollins, 2009).

5 Donald Miller, *Blue Like Jazz* (Nashville, TN: Thomas Nelson, 2003), 113–27.

CHAPTER NINE: KEPT OCCUPIED BY GOD

1 Annie S. Hawks, "I Need Thee Every Hour," 1872.
2 See Isa. 14:20; Jer. 8:2; 22:19.
3 Philip Graham Ryken, *Ecclesiastes: Why Everything Matters* (Wheaton, IL: Crossway, 2010), 177.
4 "St. Louis police: Jennings man shot uncle to death over pork steaks," *St. Louis Post-Dispatch*, http://www.stltoday.com/news/local/crime-and-courts/st-louis-police-jennings-man-shot-uncle-to-death-over/article_a281ed60-fc21-11e1-b1fc-001a4bcf6878.html (accessed October 1, 2012).

CHAPTER TEN: LEADERSHIP

1 Wendell Berry, *Jayber Crow: A Novel* (New York: Counterpoint, 2000), 233.
2 Ibid., 182.
3 Ibid., 187.
4 The Westminster Confession of Faith, 27.3.
5 Berry, *Jayber Crow*, 181.
6 Annie Dillard, *The Writing Life* (New York: HarperPerennial, 1990), 18.
7 See J. D. Douglas, ed., *New Bible Dictionary*, 2nd ed. (Leicester, UK: InterVarsity, 1985), 1121–25.
8 Juris Rubenis and Maris Subacs, *Finding God in a Tangled World: Thoughts and Parables* (Brewster, MA: Paraclete Press, 2007), 98.
9 John Bunyan, *The Pilgrim's Progress* (New York: Barnes & Noble Classics, 2005), 90.
10 Ibid., 91.

CHAPTER ELEVEN: RECOVERING OUR PURPOSE

1 Martin Scorsese, *Hugo* (Paramount Pictures, October 2011).
2 See The Westminster Confession of Faith, 20.1.
3 Philip Graham Ryken, *Ecclesiastes: Why Everything Matters* (Wheaton, IL: Crossway, 2010), 278.
4 Benedicta Ward, *The Desert Fathers: Sayings of the Early Christian Monks* (New York: Penguin Classics, 2003), 10.
5 John Bunyan, *Pilgrim's Progress* (New York: Barnes & Noble Classics, 2005), 175–76.
6 Ryken, *Ecclesiastes*, 279.

BIBLIOGRAPHY

Augustine. "Homilies on the Psalms." In *Augustine of Hippo: Selected Writings*. Translated by Mary T. Clark. The Classics of Western Spirituality. Mahwah, NJ: Paulist Press, 1984.

Austin, Mary. *The Land of Little Rain*. Carlisle, MA: Applewood, 2000.

Benedict. *The Rule of Saint Benedict*. New York: Penguin Classics, 2008.

Berry, Wendell. *Jayber Crow: A Novel*. New York: Counterpoint, 2000.

———. *A Continuous Harmony: Essays Cultural and Agricultural*. Washington, DC: Shoemaker & Hoard, 1972.

Bridges, Charles. *Ecclesiastes*. Edinburgh: The Banner of Truth, 1960.

Brother Lawrence. *The Practice of the Presence of God*. New Kensington, PA: Whitaker House, 1982.

Brown, William P. *Ecclesiastes*. Louisville, KY: John Knox, 2000.

Bunyan, John. *The Pilgrim's Progress*. New York: Barnes & Noble Classics, 2005.

Calvin, John. *Institutes of the Christian Religion*. Edited by John T. McNeill. Translated by Ford Lewis Battles. The Library of Christian Classics. Philadelphia: Westminster Press, 1960.

———. *Institutes of the Christian Religion*. 2 vols. Translated by Henry Beveridge. Edinburgh: Calvin Translation Society, 1845.

Carson, Mike. "The Keeper's Voice." In *The Keeper's Voice*. Baton Rouge, LA: Louisiana State University Press, 2010.

Cohen, Kerry. *Loose Girl: A Memoir of Promiscuity*. New York: Hyperion, 2008. Quoted in https://www.kirkusreviews.com/book-reviews/kerry-cohen/loose-girl/#review (accessed October 1, 2012).

Curtis, Edward M., and John J. Brugaletta, *Discovering the Way of Wisdom: Spirituality in the Wisdom Literature*. Grand Rapids: Kregel, 2004.

Dillard, Annie. *The Writing Life*. New York: HarperPerennial, 1990.

Douglas, J. D., ed. *New Bible Dictionary*. 2nd ed. Leicester, UK: Inter-Varsity, 1985.

Eaton, Michael A. *Ecclesiastes*. Tyndale Old Testament Commentary. Downers Grove, IL: InterVarsity, 2009.

Eswine, Zack. *Preaching to a Post-Everything World: Crafting Biblical Sermons That Connect with Our Culture*. Grand Rapids: Baker, 2008.

———. "Sage Preaching for Postmodern Contexts." *Reformation & Revival Journal* 14 (2005).

Faggen, Robert, ed. *Striving Towards Being: The Letters of Thomas Merton and Czeslaw Milosz*. New York: Farrar, Straus & Giroux, 1997.

Fox, Michael V. *A Time to Tear Down and a Time to Build Up: A Re-Reading of Ecclesiastes*. Grand Rapids: Eerdmans, 2009.

Frost, Robert. "A Line-Storm Song." In *Everyman's Library*. Edited by John Hollander. New York: Alfred A. Knopf, 1997.

Goulston, Mark. "Why Are Americans So Unhappy?" http://www.huffingtonpost.com/mark-goulston-md/why-are-americans-so-unha_b_1112384.html (accessed November 25, 2011).

Gray, Thomas. "Elegy Written in a Country Church Yard." http://www.poets.org/viewmedia.php/prmMID/19371 (accessed December 15, 2011).

Greidanus, Sidney. *Preaching Christ from Ecclesiastes: Foundations for Expository Sermons*. Grand Rapids: Eerdmans, 2010.

Hass, Robert. "Iowa January." In *The Apple Trees at Olema: New and Selected Poems*. New York: HarperCollins, 2010.

Hecht, Jennifer Michael. *Doubt: A History*. New York: Harper-SanFrancisco, 2004.

Herbert, George. "The Temple." In *George Herbert: The Complete English Works*. New York: Alfred A. Knopf, 1995.

Kreeft, Peter. *Three Philosophies of Life*. San Francisco, CA: Ignatius Press, 1989.

Larkin, Philip. "Church Going." In *The Less Deceived*. Hessle, East Yorkshire: The Marvel Press, 1955.

Lewis, C. S. *A Grief Observed*. London: Faber and Faber, 1961.

———. *The Weight of Glory and Other Addresses*. New York: HarperCollins, 2001.

Lobdell, William. *Losing My Religion: How I Lost My Faith Reporting on Religion in America—and Found Unexpected Peace*. New York: HarperCollins, 2009.

Longman, Tremper. *The Book of Ecclesiastes*. The New International Commentary on the Old Testament. Grand Rapids: Eerdmans, 1998.

McCarthy, Cormac. *The Stonemason: A Play in Five Acts*. New York: Vintage, 1998.

Miller, Donald. *Blue Like Jazz*. Nashville, TN: Thomas Nelson, 2003.

O'Connor, Flannery. "A Good Man Is Hard to Find." In *The Complete Stories*. New York: Farrar, Straus and Giroux, 1971.

Packer, J. I. *Knowing God*. Downers Grove, IL: InterVarsity, 1993.

Rubenis, Juris, and Maris Subacs. *Finding God in a Tangled World: Thoughts and Parables*. Brewster, MA: Paraclete Press, 2007.

Ryken, Philip Graham. *Ecclesiastes: Why Everything Matters*. Wheaton, IL: Crossway, 2010.

Savatar, Fernando. *The Questions of Life: An Invitation to Philosophy*. Malden, MA: Blackwell Publishers, 2002.

Schaeffer, Francis. *Death in the City*. Wheaton, IL: Crossway, 2002.

———. *Letters of Francis A. Schaeffer: Spiritual Reality in the Personal Christian Life*. Wheaton, IL: Crossway, 1985.

Shenk, Joshua Wolf. *Lincoln's Melancholy: How Depression Challenged a President and Fueled His Greatness*. New York: Houghton Mifflin, 2005.

Stevens, Wallace. "Adagia." In *Opus Posthumus: Poems, Plays, Prose*. New York: Vintage, 1990.

"St. Louis police: Jennings man shot uncle to death over pork steaks." *St. Lewis Post-Dispatch.* http://www.stltoday.com /news/local/crime-and-courts/st-louis-police-jennings -man-shot-uncle-to-death-over/article_a281ed60-fc21–11e1 -b1fc-001a4bcf6878.html (accessed October 1, 2012).

Stott, John. *Between Two Worlds: The Art of Preaching in the 20th Century.* Grand Rapids: Eerdmans, 1982.

Ten Boom, Corrie. *The Hiding Place.* Grand Rapids: Chosen, 1971.

Tolkien, J. R. R. *The Fellowship of the Ring.* Boston: Houghton Mifflin, 1987.

Ward, Benedicta. *The Desert Fathers: Sayings of the Early Christian Monks.* New York: Penguin Classics, 2003.

Wilde, Oscar. *The Picture of Dorian Gray.* New York: Modern Library, 1992.

Wolterstorff, Nicolas. *Lament for a Son.* Grand Rapids: Eerdmans, 1987.

INDEX OF SCRIPTURE